Marriage in the Nude

Marriage in the Nude

A MAN'S GUIDE TO LOVE AND GRACE

Dr. Ritchie Miller

Library of Congress Cataloguing-in-Publication Data
Miller, Ritchie

ISBN: 1546748261
ISBN 13: 9781546748267

Contents

Introduction

God used a naked woman to show men how to have a great marriage.

Now if you are like most men, I already have your attention. But it is true. God used a beautiful woman who was as naked as the day she was created to demonstrate His love, grace, and purpose for humanity. You've got to love a Creator who introduces His plan like that! Intrigued? Well, it gets better.

When Adam first saw Eve, he was overwhelmed. I think he had good reason to be. She was the most beautiful woman on earth. She was naked. And she was his! I love his response when he first saw Eve. He said, "At last!" I imagine after having seen elephants, donkeys, jackals, and everything in-between he was more than ready to see a real, live woman. His point of exclamation demonstrates just how wonderful, beautiful, and mysteriously joyful marriage was meant to be. Adam waxed poetic when he declared, "she is bone of my bone and flesh of my flesh." Men have written poems and songs for the women they love ever since. Come on! What man wouldn't do everything in his power to woo her? She was perfect. She was more than he ever dreamed. She was for him alone, and they both knew it. Did I mention that she was naked?

In Genesis, we find that the creation account demonstrates God love, blessing, and purpose for us. It is a picture of God's grace to us. Grace is God's eternal purpose for humanity. It is undeserved, unearned, unmerited kindness and favor from God. Adam certainly did not do anything to deserve God's favor, but God richly and freely poured out His grace on the first humans, because that is who God is. Before there was any sin, there was grace! That was God's original foundation for marriage and all human relationships. A marriage that is grace-centered functions the way God intends all marriages to function – centered on a relationship with God and built on His grace.

Marriage and human sexuality show God's beautiful, creative purpose and His mandate for humanity - produce worshippers of God Almighty. He blessed everything beyond our capacity to comprehend. Amid that amazing creation, we find that the man and the woman were "naked and were not ashamed."

What a powerful statement. Adam and Eve were naked. There was no covering up. He and she were open, intimate, and completely vulnerable to each other's love. They hid nothing. The power of their connection must have been stunning. There were no secret agendas. No lies. No deceit. No manipulation. No using or abusing each other for devious purposes. It was just pure, naked marriage. It overflowed with grace and love. It had an unlimited capacity for pleasure, connection, intimacy, and purpose because it was grace-centered. It was marriage in the nude.

Over the next several chapters I aim to show you how God can empower you to have that kind of relationship with your spouse. His plan for your marriage is greater than you have imagined. I realize that you can't have a perfect home life. After all, both you and your spouse are imperfect people. But you can have a happy marriage. You can live by God's values and have a home filled with love. You are not perfect, but you are getting better and growing when you follow Jesus by faith and live in the fullness of His grace. You can have a little slice of what they had in the Garden of Eden before they sinned. You can have the powerful bond that makes you one.

But first, you must get naked.

PART ONE

The Naked Truth About Men and Marriage

Guys, let's be honest for a second. Our modern culture doesn't celebrate real, biblical manliness. Men often get labeled as knuckle-dragging Neanderthals whose only motivation in life consists of the next sexual exploit and the next sandwich. We often elevate fatally flawed heroes who exhibit the kind of behavior that propagates the stereotypes but falls far short of satisfying the God-given desires and drives of godly men. It does not help that many resources aimed at women portray the ideal man as one who is in touch with his feminine side, who loves to sit with the girls with his legs folded under him, and loves talking about his feelings.

God has created you as a man to live in His image and to fulfill His grand purpose. He has given you natural desires - a sex drive, the desire to protect, provide and lead – for a holy purpose. When these desires get harnessed for God's glory, they empower you to be the kind of man that He wants you to be. Can unharnessed desires become harmful? Of course, but when you commit your life to God and His grand purpose, you become the best version of a man and a husband.

In this section, we will discover the naked truth about men and marriage. We will look at the most important thing about you and your relationship with your wife.

DAY ONE

A Man's Greatest Priority

Over many years of being in ministry, I have heard people talk a lot about what is most important to them. I imagine that most people want to sound sincere and spiritual when talking to a pastor. Most Christians with whom I speak say their relationship with God and their relationship with their family are the most important things in their lives. However, I have discovered that saying something is a priority does not always make it a priority. You know your priorities by what you do rather than what you say. If I say that my relationship with God and my family are the most important things in my life, then my actions must support that, or I am simply fooling myself.

I believe that most followers of Christ want their relationship with God and their family to come first. It is just that they don't know how to make them a priority. Just because you go to church does not mean that Jesus is preeminent. Just because you love your family does not mean that your wife and children always take precedence in your actions. Your job, running a household, managing a career, getting the kids to school, and other good things clamor for your attention. These actions are necessary. They are a part of living a normal life. God gives us these things to bless us. But they, too often, steal first place in our lives because of the time they demand. And it is not as if we can live without jobs, households, and schedules. Nor should we. So how do we make the *most important* things predominant in our lives? How do we keep the *main thing* the *main thing*?

What You Believe about God is the Most Important Thing about Your Marriage

How you see God determines everything in your life. If you are an atheist, your beliefs, actions, priorities, and life-plan will reflect the fact that you don't believe in God. You won't see God as gracious and loving. You won't live like you are accountable to Him. As a result, your attitude and actions will make evident your beliefs. What you believe about God determines how you live.

If you are like many Christians and see God as the Big-Guy-With-The-Heavenly-Stick, you will live in fear and defeat. You see God as the overbearing, under-concerned Deity that is waiting to hit you upside the head every time He gets a chance. Instead of believing the truth of Jesus, you believe the lies of the devil. You will live as a list keeper. You believe that God is only pleased when you get an "A" on your heavenly report card. You will live in frustration because you can never do enough, or pray enough, or give enough to measure up. Often people who see God like this become hypocritical or hypercritical. They become hypocrites when they try to approach God based on their good deeds. They get an over-inflated sense of their righteousness when others do not keep the same list of rules they do. They become hypercritical because they see God as a stern taskmaster. Instead of living out of love, they criticize anyone and everything. This kind of Christianity often damages the cause of Christ. Non-Christians see it as overbearing, self-righteous, and mean-spirited. They are correct. God designed us to flesh out the gospel through his grace, not live by a code of self-righteous morality. What you believe about God is the most important thing about you.

If you see God as the Bible describes Him, then you will live accordingly. If you see Him as righteous and a loving giver of grace, then your life and beliefs will reflect that. Realizing that your works aren't the source of your blessing changes your attitude. Once you discover that God's unearned, undeserved, and unmerited grace is the fountain of all that is good in your life, then you behave differently. If you believe that the "great exchange" at the cross – our sins for his righteousness - is what brings His favor and kindness, then you perceive God differently. When you believe that about God, it changes the way you live. It affects your behavior and your attitude. It improves your marriage!

Talk with Your Wife

1. *What is your image of God? Do you see him as a loving giver of grace, or do you see Him as a demanding taskmaster?*
2. *What is your image of a human father? From your experience, do you think of him as being disappointed, demanding, harsh, uncaring, or uninvolved? Do you see him as a loving, providing, encouraging, and grace-filled person?*
3. *Does the image of your earthly father affect your image of the Heavenly Father?*
4. *What kind of father do you want to be?*
5. *Pray together with your wife. Ask God to empower you to believe who He is and that you will reflect that in your marriage.*

DAY TWO

A Husband's Role in Understanding Grace

Do you recall the story that Jesus told in Matthew 18[1] about the king and his servants? One servant owed him ten thousand talents. According to some scholars, this would be the equivalent of ten billion dollars in today's currency! It was an enormous amount that was on the very edge of what people in the ancient world could conceive about money. The servant could not possibly pay it back. But the king, in love and grace, completely forgave the debt. What an act of grace!

But this same servant went out and grabbed a fellow servant by the throat and demanded that he pay back immediately what he owed him. The amount he owed was probably between five and ten thousand dollars in today's currency. In comparison to what he owed the king, it was a million times less! Well, the story goes on and tells us that the forgiven servant threw his fellow servant into debtor's prison until he could pay back the comparatively small sum. When the king heard about it, he was enraged and delivered this man to the "tormentors," signifying the torture that having an unforgiving spirit brings.

Do you get the point? Jesus teaches us that the sins we have committed against the Heavenly Father are far greater than any wrong done to us. God forgave us more than we can imagine; therefore, we must forgive others. Our understanding of God's forgiveness defines our lives. Rather than seeing himself as a debtor who received forgiveness for an unforgivable debt, the man in the story

1 Matthew 18:21-35, The Parable of the Unforgiving Servant

lived as a collector of debts owed to him. When you and I fail to see the depth of God's forgiveness, then we also live as collectors rather than debtors. The result is torment. If you think your spouse owes you because of his or her actions, it leads to a marriage that rivals the torments of hell. Love, joy, peace, and blessing eschew that marriage. What you believe about God is the most important thing about your relationship because it will determine whether you are a debtor or a collector. People who live by grace recognize that God has forgiven them far more than they can ever forgive another human. As a result, they are empowered by the gospel to live and forgive accordingly.

Putting Jesus at the Center of Your Marriage Brings Grace

Having Christ at the center of your relationship is essential for God's blessings. Many Christians think about priorities as a list of descending concerns. Whatever gets listed first is most important and gets the most attention. As you go down the list, each item receives less attention and time. The problem with this kind of thinking is that it makes Jesus and your family boxes that you check off your list.

The better way to see it is to make Jesus the center of your life. Things at the center don't get treated as a "to-do" list, but they permeate everything.

My goal is not to give you a list of do's and don'ts. I want to show you the heart of Jesus. What Jesus came to do was to ravage our old, dead spirit and give us new life through God's radical grace. My intention is not to point a finger or beat you up over your failures. I want to focus you on your future, not your past. I want you to believe in the hope that we have through the grace of Jesus. His grace is necessary for salvation, but it is also crucial for Christian living. I want to show you how you can have a deep sense of happiness and oneness through Jesus. I love marriage as a concept and an institution. I relish what good marriages do for families and culture. When you make Jesus the center of your family, you can have a home life that is blessed beyond your wildest dreams!

You have heard it said that good marriages take work. I certainly believe that is true - to a degree. You are not perfect. Neither is your spouse because everyone has a sin nature. You can't have a perfect marriage, but you can have a Christ-centered marriage that is blessed by God and happy. You can't neglect your home life and expect it to be great.

Your marriage needs God's grace more than it needs your work. How many people do you know that have said they work hard on their relationship, but it is still bad? Jesus can do in a short time what would take us a lifetime to do. I am not suggesting that you can say a magic prayer and never worry about your marriage again. However, I am saying that God's grace applies to more than our salvation. It applies to every part of our lives, including the husband/wife relationship. Remember that Jesus performed His first miracle at a wedding. He turned water to wine, which represents the grace of God. His grace can help you too!

Talk with Your Wife

1. *God's grace is His unearned, unmerited, undeserved kindness and favor to us. Do you ever struggle with feeling like you must earn God's favor by the good things you do? Do you ever feel like you do not deserve God's love?*
2. *Living with a forgiving spirit is essential to living with God's grace. By reminding ourselves of how much He has forgiven us, we can extend forgiveness to others. Do you need to ask your wife for forgiveness for something you have done? Ask her now. In your conversation and prayer together, allow her to ask for your forgiveness too.*
3. *What areas of your marriage need work? How can living with grace improve that area?*
4. *Pray together and ask God to reveal His grace to you and your wife and let you both see His grace is a greater way.*

DAY THREE

How Men Can Put Jesus at the Center of Their Marriage

Putting Jesus at the center of your married life sounds spiritual, but it can also seem vague and out of reach for most people. It is a Christian-sounding thing that we like to say, but can't quite explain when it comes to applying it to our daily lives. It sounds good but how do you do it? How do you measure it? How do you know if you have put Jesus at the center of your marriage? Let's look at the first marriage in the Bible and find out God's plan for you.

"Therefore a man shall leave his father and his mother and hold fast to his wife, and they shall become one flesh. And the man and his wife were both naked and were not ashamed." [2]

These verses are part of the creation story, and they show us God's blueprint from the very beginning. They demonstrate how we are to put Christ and His grace at the center of our marriage.

Becoming One

The word "one" in the phrase "one flesh" is the same word used in Deuteronomy 6:4 "Hear, O Israel, The Lord our God, the Lord is one."[3] What does it mean when it states, "The Lord (Yahweh) is one?" It means God is complete or whole. He has no need because he is perfect as Father, Son, and Holy Spirit. In the same way, we can only be complete or whole in marriage through faith in Jesus. When we are

2 Genesis 2:24-25, ESV

3 Deuteronomy 6:4

"in" Jesus, we are ready to become one flesh. Your life is to revolve around Jesus, not a man or woman.

Since God is one and He wants husband and wife to be one in Him, we must view our marriage as God does. It is quite common for people to describe marriage as two halves that make a whole. According to the Bible, no husband or wife is a half-person looking for their other half-person to make a complete entity. The biblical definition of personhood and marriage is not one plus one equals one. God's formula is that you and your spouse must find wholeness by joining one plus one plus one. You can only be complete and unified when both husband and wife have a relationship with Jesus. You are one by keeping Jesus at the center of your marriage. *God's math for oneness in marriage is one plus one plus one equals one.*

God gave marriage to show us the relationship between Jesus and the Church. It shows how much He loves us. God brought the woman from the man's side. The church was born from Jesus' side on the cross. Marriage teaches us about God and Jesus. The first step to becoming complete or whole in marriage is for the husband and wife to declare his and her faith in Jesus for salvation and their home.

If you are to keep Jesus at the center of your marriage, you must place your faith in the finished work of Christ. Many people believe that being a Christian means being moral. They think those who are good go to heaven. But the Bible shows us we can't be good enough on our own. "For all have sinned and fall short of the glory of God." [4]

Following Christ is about a relationship with God, not a list of rules. "Jesus said to him, 'I am the way, the truth, and the life. No one comes to the Father, except through me.'" [5]

Becoming a follower of Christ doesn't depend on our good deeds, but on what Jesus did for us when He died on the cross. Jesus took our punishment and gave us a way to be forgiven and made right with God. That is Good News! We can only experience this through our faith in Jesus. Through our faith, God gives us his undeserved, unmerited, unearned favor. "For by grace you have been saved through faith. And this is not your own doing; it is the gift of God, not a result of works, so that no one may boast." [6]

Following Christ is a matter of faith. Through faith in Jesus you admit you have sinned and then ask God to forgive you. "If we confess our sins, he is faithful and just to forgive us our sins and to cleanse us from all unrighteousness." [7]

By believing in Christ's death and resurrection, you admit to God that you need Him. "If you confess with your

---

4 Romans 3:23

5 John 14:6

6 Ephesians 2:8-9

7 1 John 1:9

mouth that Jesus is Lord and believe in your heart that God raised him from the dead, you will be saved." [8]

Accepting God's gift of salvation is as simple as inviting Jesus Christ to come into your life. By doing this, you admit that you believe God's promise to save you. You trust in the finished work of Christ. Salvation does not come through your goodness or morality. This act of faith is the most important step for putting Christ at the center of your marriage. Only when you trust Him for salvation and forgiveness can you trust Him with your family relationships.

God loves you more than you can comprehend. He has a plan for your life. He has a purpose for your life. You are not an accident! He promises that He will never leave you and that He will always be there for you no matter what. He will be there for you in your marriage when you trust in Him.

"Do not be afraid or discouraged, for the Lord will personally go ahead of you. He will be with you; he will neither fail you nor abandon you." [9]

Faith

Putting Jesus at the center of your marriage requires faith. We must trust His promise to be with us and help us in every circumstance of life. We must trust God's power to

8 Romans 10:9

9 Deuteronomy 31:8, NLT

make us complete in Him. The Holy Spirit can transform you. If He saved your soul, then He can save your marriage. God's grace can do more in a moment than you can do with a lifetime of work. Doubt limits every part of your life, but faith sees limitless possibilities through Jesus.

Purpose

When we keep Jesus at the center of our married life and trust in God's grace, we fulfill God's purpose for marriage. God's purpose unquestionably included companionship, fellowship, sexual intimacy, and procreation. But I do not believe that was the primary reason He created humanity and the institution of marriage. God made us in His image, and as God's unique creation, we were created to have a relationship with God! Being an image-bearer means we are God's representatives and that He designed us from the beginning to take His image and message throughout the earth and fill the earth with worshippers of Him. Only a grace-centered, Christ-centered marriage can fulfill that purpose.

Anything not used for its defined purpose gets abused. For example, a shoe is designed to be worn as apparel for feet, not to hammer nails. I have used a shoe to hit a nail. I imagine you probably have tried to channel your inner carpenter through this ill-advised technique, too. Nevertheless, using something for a purpose for which it was never intended leads to abuse and unnecessary damage. The same is true with marriage. When you don't follow God's original plan, your relationship deteriorates. At worst, you will descend into communication problems, abuse, neglect, and potentially divorce. At best, your marriage will never reach its potential.

Talk with Your Wife

1. *Do you feel like you are "one" in your marriage? Talk about some areas where you need to be more united.*
2. *Have you both trusted in Christ alone as your Savior? Share your story with each other, even if you both know the story. It will be a great encouragement to one other.*
3. *Where do you both need to grow in your faith? What could you do to increase your faith and make it stronger?*
4. *What do you believe your purpose in life is? Share with each other how you can help each other fulfill that purpose.*
5. *Pray together for God to increase your faith and your understanding of his purpose.*

DAY FOUR

Building a Blessed Marriage

In the creation account found in Genesis[10] chapters 1-3 we see a powerful and important concept about the relationship between husband and wife. After God had created the universe, the world, and people, He did something significant. Genesis 1:28 states, "And God blessed them." Before He ever gave them a command, He blessed them. What a picture of his grace! God demonstrates that His blessing and grace do not come because of our good deeds. Grace is essential for marriage. If we learn to work from God's blessing rather than for God's blessing, we position ourselves for God to do more than we could ever do on our own.

Understanding the concept of God's unmerited, unearned, and undeserved favor is a fundamental truth by which we must live. Only when we recognize His grace can we joyfully and truthfully obey Him. All his commands are rooted in His love for us. It is only through His grace - not our human effort - that we can live a blessed life and enjoy God's favor.

In the creation story, God gave three blessings and three commands. He blessed the creation, He blessed humans, and He blessed the Sabbath. Then He commanded Adam and Eve to fill the earth, to subdue the earth, and to have dominion over it.

You could say that God blessed work, relationships, and worship. Of course, we know how the story ends.

10 Genesis chapters 1-3

Adam and Eve sinned. Because of sin, God placed a curse on the earth, our work, and our relationships. Sin not only obstructed our fellowship with God, but it also caused us to die spiritually. We inherited Adams' sin nature and are born separated from God and in need of a Redeemer. God initially blessed work, relationships, and worship. Through Jesus, He can redeem your marriage, your job, and your spirit. We come alive and receive God's blessing because we trust His grace.

Have you ever considered what the first commands were? He told Adam and Eve to have a lot of sex – be fruitful and multiply. We are commanded to be productive and prolific with our lives, and we are called to fill the earth with worshippers. Doesn't that show us that God's original purpose was rooted in the gospel? He told them to take care of the planet. Humans were to be productive and blessed in their work. Next, He told the first married couple to have dominion over creation. They were to provide leadership and to rule like kings and queens over everything. They were to carry out God's purpose. As a bonus, He told them to eat a lot of food and to enjoy the pleasures of God. You've got to love the fact that God's first commands were to have sex and to enjoy delicious food! Do you get the idea that God wants to bless you?

The key to understanding all of this is to understand God's original intention and purpose. That purpose is God's desire for you today. The original Hebrew word for "blessed"[11] shows us what God wants us to do. Most of the time that word is translated as "blessed," and it describes God's incredible blessing and grace to us. But several times in the Old Testament the word is translated "kneel" or "praise." The purpose of God's blessing is for you to worship Him!

We worship what we love. The Bible overflows with stories of people who worshiped anything but God. They venerated themselves, sex, the creation, and just about anything you can imagine. But the whole purpose of creation was for us to worship God and have a relationship with Him. God's Divine Order was for our worship to flow from His blessing as a response to His amazing love. It is firmly rooted in His grace. We don't worship because of our work, but because of God's work. We don't receive grace because of our actions, but because of God's actions. When we get it out of order, we do the same things that Adam and Eve did. We sin, we question God's love and purpose, and we lose intimacy and connection with God. We replace it with worry, fear, communication breakdown, finger pointing, blame shifting, and problems with work, marriage, and children. In short, we live in sin and worship our ability and our efforts. We get the results of our human effort. Those efforts always fall short of God's standard. In the end, worship of self and created things lead to death. Death is always the result of any human effort that

11 James Strong, *Enhanced Strong's Lexicon*, #1288 (Woodside Bible Fellowship, 1995).

separates itself from God's grace. Spiritual death. Physical death. And even the death of our marriage.

But thank God for His grace! Living from grace instead of trying to earn God's grace transforms our lives. As a result, it changes our marriage. Grace is the foundation for a blessed marriage!

Talk with Your Wife

1. *How can you work from God's blessing rather than for God's blessing in your marriage?*
2. *What does it reveal to you about the nature of God that His first commands to Adam and Eve were to have sex and to enjoy delicious food?*
3. *How do you think a better understanding of worshipping God can improve your marriage, work, and parenting?*
4. *How do you think worship and enjoying God's blessings can improve your sex life?*
5. *Pray together for God to help you both to live from God's blessing rather than for God's blessing in your marriage.*

PART TWO

The Naked Truth About Your Words

During my freshman year of college, a friend and I hung out one night in a commons area on our campus. He played football and tipped the scales at over 400 pounds. With a grin on his face, he said, "Hey, Ritchie, watch this." He backed up about twenty feet and started running at a large couch. I thought he was going to tackle it. As he sprinted (OK it was more like a violent waddle) toward the innocent couch, his steely determination told me he was planning to do something ill-advised. He intended to jump over the sofa. All four hundred pounds of a buffing, charging, jiggling man. His graceful form and athleticism surprised me. To my surprise, he cleared the back of the sofa. It felt like a super slow motion highlight on Sports Center. He had the eye of the tiger. His face forged with purpose. His feet lifted high in the air.

He almost made it.

I will never forget what it was like to watch his foot tear through the seat like a hot knife through butter. He wore the couch around his lower leg. Panic-filled eyes searched the room for help and understanding, but he found none. He destroyed valuable college property with dramatic flair. He pulled his foot out, bent over, and picked up the injured piece of furniture. The last thing I saw, between hysterical gasps for air, was the behemoth carrying the couch out of the room under one arm.

Some couples are like my friend when it comes to communication in marriage. They huff and puff and they almost make it. In the end, all they accomplish is ruining some furniture. In this section, my goal is to help you learn how to use grace-filled words to build your marriage. Hopefully, it will save some innocent furniture too.

DAY FIVE

How You Talk to Your Wife Matters

There is a stark contrast between the words Adam spoke to Eve before The Fall and his words about her after he sinned. Before he sinned, his words dripped with purpose, faith, romance, and grace. They were uplifting words that built her spirit and filled her with joy. "Then the LORD God made a woman from the rib, and he brought her to the man. 'At last!' the man exclaimed. 'This one is bone from my bone, and flesh from my flesh! She will be called woman, because she was taken from man.'"[12]

After he had sinned, he called her "the woman you gave me."[13] No doubt these words were filled with contempt, sarcasm, and criticism. They were words of blame and were meant to demean and tear her down. The disparity in his words demonstrates the difference between grace-filled words and graceless words.

The Power of Your Words

When a marriage gets built on God's grace, your words reflect it. In Ephesians chapter four the Apostle Paul writes about the change that happens to us when we place our faith in Christ. When we experience God's saving grace, the result is a new life and a new power within us to exhibit God's grace to others. We experience the power of Christ to renew our minds and change our ways. Because Christ lives in us, Paul proclaims that we practice a new way of living and speaking. Through the power of the indwelling

12 Genesis 2:22-23, NLT

13 Genesis 3:12

Christ, we can communicate the truth in love. His Spirit helps us deal with our anger and bitterness. We use our words to build up, become concerned for the well-being of others, and stop using words that foster arguments and tear down. Our language transforms, and we become kind and forgiving. In verse 29 he uses a phrase that I believe captures the essence of how a Christ follower is to talk. He states that the purpose of our words is to "give grace to those who hear."[14] Our words have power, and they reveal what is going in our spiritual lives.

Grace-Filled Words Require Faith

Trusting Jesus is necessary for His becoming the center of your marriage. The words you say must be rooted in your faith. They reflect the reality of your relationship with Christ. Faith grows with our words and our declarations. It begins with words and actions throughout the Bible. In other words, it is not real faith until we say it or act on it. Romans 10:9-13 shows us how our words connect to our faith.

> **If you openly declare** that Jesus is Lord and believe in your heart that God raised him from the dead, you will be saved. For it is by believing in your heart that you are made right with God, and it is **by openly declaring your faith** that you are saved. As the Scriptures tell us, "Anyone who trusts in him will never be disgraced." Jew and Gentile

14 Ephesians 4:29

> are the same in this respect. They have the same Lord, who gives generously to all who call on him. For "**Everyone who calls on the name of the LORD will be saved**."[15] (Emphasis added)

Notice the emphasis on declaring your faith by the words you say. It is important to your marriage that you use grace-filled and faith-filled words. Our words announce our faith. Even if the things you say have not happened yet, then you can declare in faith that your spouse will become what God has called him or her to be. We say these things in faith, believing that God will make them real according to His will. Speak words over your spouse and children that declare God's goodness, purpose, and blessing in their lives. Abraham believed this and God blessed him for it.

> That is why it depends on faith, in order that the promise may rest on grace and be guaranteed to all his offspring—not only to the adherent of the law but also to the one who shares the faith of Abraham, who is the father of us all, as it is written, "I have made you the father of many nations"—in the presence of the God in whom he believed, who gives life to the dead **and calls into existence the things that do not exist**. In hope he believed against hope, that he should become the father of many nations, as he had been told, "So shall your offspring be." He did not weaken in faith when he considered his own body, which was as good

15 Romans 10:9-13

> as dead (since he was about a hundred years old), or when he considered the barrenness of Sarah's womb. No unbelief made him waver concerning the promise of God, but he grew strong in his faith as he gave glory to God, fully convinced that God was able to do what he had promised. That is why his faith was "counted to him as righteousness."[16] (Emphasis added)

Keeping Jesus at the center of your marriage gives you the strength to speak words of grace and faith. There is great power in your words when they demonstrate your trust in God.

Once again, we see this in the creation story. Adam waxed poetic when he first saw Eve. *"At last!" the man exclaimed.* "This one is bone from my bone and flesh from my flesh! She will be called 'woman,' for she was taken from 'man.'"[17] Can you imagine how excited he was to see her? He just laid eyes on the most beautiful woman in the world, and she was all his. But don't miss the faith in his words. He declared that God created them both. He recognized God's creative purpose. He admitted that God gave them both a beautiful gift and this gift demonstrated their union in God. What a powerful declaration of faith!

What came next also showed a great understanding of the importance of trusting God. "Therefore a man shall

16 Romans 4:16-22

17 Genesis 2:23

leave his father and his mother and hold fast to his wife, and they shall become one flesh."[18] Adam believed that their union was only complete when they had a relationship with God. His powerful words acknowledged that the primary focus in marriage must be toward God. God wants you to have a Jesus-centered family life. Your words matter to your spouse and God. How you intertwine faith in your marital communication directly affects your awareness of God's blessings.

18 Genesis 2:24, ESV

Talk with Your Wife

1. *How can both husband and wife speak more graciously to each other? Talk about it.*
2. *How can you depend on Christ to empower your words to each other?*
3. *Faith-filled words matter. What can you speak in faith <u>over</u> your spouse that will build up? What can you say in faith <u>to</u> your spouse that will build up?*
4. *The Bible teaches that the Word of God increases our faith. How do daily Bible reading and prayer help you speak grace-filled words to each other?*
5. *Pray together. Ask God to help you both grow in faith and speak graciously toward each other.*

DAY SIX

Speak Man, But Be Fluent in Woman

Does it ever seem like males and females use the same words and yet speak entirely different languages? Welcome to the world of marriage. You must understand that husbands and wives speak differently. That is OK because God designed it that way for a purpose. Learning to build your lives on the foundation of God's grace will help you become fluent in the way your spouse speaks and become a better communicator.

Couples are to be one in Jesus without losing their unique individuality. Understanding this can help you navigate the sometimes-rough waters of marriage. God made men and women differently. We all know that. Truthfully, the differences are what attract us to each other. Nonetheless, in the same way that the differences can captivate us, they can also frustrate us. They can cause friction in the best relationship.

The Hebrew word describing Adam's creation means, "to squeeze out."[19] I think this helps us understand how a man operates and thinks. Ladies, your husband came from dirt and is more comfortable being dirty, hunting, and doing other manly pursuits like playing football. He is less refined than you. He can be crude. That may explain why a man will share a foul smell with another man and laugh about it. It also helps us understand the makeup of the male sex. Guys handle and express emotions differently than women. I believe God made men tougher on the outside and less connected to their feelings. They need to be

19 Strong's Hebrew Concordance, #3335

this way to protect their family. They have a God-given aggression that is useful in providing for a family. It is important for a wife to know how God created her husband because it will help her appreciate the differences in the way he communicates and expresses himself. Just because your husband may not cry as easily as you do during a kitten commercial does not mean he has no emotions. He just processes them differently.

When God created Eve, He took her from Adam's side. The Hebrew word used to describe God's creation of woman means, "to build carefully and skillfully or to fashion her."[20] God seemed to take a little more time and care in creating woman. God created Eve to be considerably more refined than Adam. Women cherish beauty and cleanliness. They communicate differently. They admire cute things. They are tougher on the inside than a man because they are more emotionally connected than a man. Although a wife's emotional makeup is entirely different from her husband's in most cases, it is equally important. In fact, it may be more important. Women are the emotional glue that holds the family together. They are more in touch with their emotions because they need to be. Wives bring beauty and romance into marriage. Moms provide a unique emotional expression to their children that is critical to their well-being. Women have a God-created skill set that men do not have. It is beautiful and necessary for

20 Francis Brown, Samuel Rolles Driver, and Charles Augustus Briggs, *Enhanced Brown-Driver-Briggs Hebrew and English Lexicon* (Oxford: Clarendon Press, 1977), 699, Genesis 2:22.

a Jesus-centered marriage. Women are emotionally stronger, more intuitive, and softer on the outside than men. Thank God! It is a part of His design.

As a pastor, I have observed that these differences are a part of what makes marriage a beautiful mystery. They bring delight and joy. However, these differences in emotional expression, communication, and instinct can also be a source of marital conflict. Many marital conflicts stem from not understanding these differences. Only when Jesus is at the center of your marriage can you navigate these differences and live in joyous union the way God intended.

By trusting God's design for us, we can celebrate the differences between husband and wife and embrace them as a part of the blissful, yet mysterious union. The Apostle Peter admonished husbands and wives to live together "in an understanding way."[21] Learning the subtle differences between the ways men and women communicate will go a long way in helping your communication with each other. Females tend to use many more words in a day than men. Males tend to use fewer words. Women have an innate desire for intimate communication. They love details! Men, on the other hand, tend to think that their actions speak for them, and usually require fewer intimate details.

I learned this early in our marriage. Kim is a naturally outgoing person. She loves to meet people, and she quickly empathizes with them. She meets total strangers and

21 1 Peter 3:7

quickly discovers details about their family, children, where they are from, and things I don't even know about some of my friends! I once played basketball with a group of men for about two years. One day Kim asked me about some of them, and I realized that I did not even know some of their last names, much less any personal details about their families. I knew their first names and what they did for a living. I knew who had a good jump shot and who played the best defense, but that was about it. It blew her mind that I never had any deep conversations with any of them. I think that illustrates the difference between the way men and women communicate. She has had to learn to understand the way I communicate. She has learned to be patient with me and has extended a lot of grace to me. She understands that just because I tend not to be detailed, does not mean that I don't care. I have had to learn to pay more attention and grow in communication skills. Engaging in deeper and longer conversations ministers to her needs in a Christ-like manner. She naturally craves conversation, and I have been mandated by God to understand her and love her as Jesus loves the church. We have both learned to know each other better, and as a result, our marriage is stronger. We are learning to celebrate our differences.

Talk with Your Wife

1. *Ask your wife how you could be a better communicator?*
2. *Tell your wife some ways that she can communicate more clearly to you.*
3. *Tell your wife that you love her. Commit to telling her that you love her every day.*
4. *Tell your wife how she can build you up using her words.*
5. *Pray with your wife. Ask God to help you both communicate to each other with grace. Assess your schedule and determine how you can spend more time together so that communication flows from being together.*

DAY SEVEN

Bless Her with Your Words

When God created something, He spoke to its source and blessed it.[22] He talked to the waters, and fish formed. He commanded the air to bring forth flying creatures, and birds were born. He told the ground to produce life, and animals appeared. None of these created things can function properly apart from their source. Fish need water. Birds need the air. Animals need the ground.

What did God do when he created man? He spoke to himself! He said, "Let us make man in our image."[23] In the same way that birds need the air, fish need the water, and animals need the ground, humanity needs Jesus. Men and women can't function properly without Him. He is our source; therefore, we must have a relationship with him to experience the greatest blessing.

To take the analogy a step further, the woman came from the man's side. Both were created in the image of God and needed God. But to help us understand how to treat each other, we must remember that God spoke to Himself when he made Adam, and then He shaped Eve from his rib. God's divine order in creation helps us understand how to treat each other in marriage. Since the Woman came from the Man's side, it makes sense that we need to be at each other's side for a blessed union. Husbands need to hug and hold their wives. She functions better when you do. She is kinder, more loving, more understanding, more fulfilled, and sexier when you do! We must operate from the source

22 Genesis 1:20-23

23 Genesis 1:26

of our blessing. We function better when we use our words to build and bless.

Words Build a Strong Foundation for Marriage

How you use words will determine how successful your marriage is. Grace-filled words help create grace-filled marriages. Without grace, you will never experience the blissful union God has in mind for you. How we speak matters.

Words are significant to the creation story. God spoke and the universe formed. God taught Adam and Eve how to talk. He not only taught them to speak, but also communicated with them. Adam used his words to name the animals.[24] Allow me to use my imagination for a moment. I think it must have been a lot of fun when he named the animals. I can imagine Adam saying, "You have four legs, you bark, and wag your tail. I think you must be a dog. You are colossal, and you have a long trunk and big floppy ears. I'll call you an elephant. You have a long neck and large spots. You look like a giraffe. Ok, who's next? Oh, I see you. You have four legs and long ears, you are insufferable and obnoxious, and you bray like a jackass. You must be an Alabama football fan!" I'm sorry, I couldn't resist.

24 Genesis 2:19-20

Grace and Your Relationship with God

When Adam first talked to Eve, you can recognize the fact that he took seriously his responsibility to extend grace to his wife. "At last!" the man exclaimed. "This one is bone from my bone and flesh from my flesh! She will be called 'woman', for she was taken from 'man.'"[25] These were beautiful words. They were words of grace. God told Adam not to eat of the wrong tree. He said this before He created Eve. Adam failed his wife because he failed to teach her, lead her, and guide her with God's Word. When he stopped talking to her, she started talking to the snake! She said something different than God said. She left off grace! When we leave grace out of the equation, we begin to feel restless and dissatisfied, and it significantly impacts our relationship with God and each other.

25 Genesis 2:23, NLT

Talk with Your Wife

1. *Take some time and tell each other what you appreciate about each other. Be specific and try to build each other up with your words.*
2. *Take a moment and share a story from your past that helped you to know that you were falling in love.*
3. *Talk about your spiritual life, church attendance, and service through your local church. Make a commitment to build your marriage through your commitment to Jesus.*
4. *Plan a date night. Commit to doing something together in the next week, even if it is small.*
5. *Hold each other and pray for God to bless your marriage.*

DAY EIGHT

Learning to Speak with God's Grace

Good communication is foundational to a successful marriage. However, poor communication is one of the most common problems in the average home. Most husbands and wives possess the ability to communicate but not the understanding of how to communicate to each other with grace. Here are a few biblical principles for communicating with God's grace.

Celebrate Each Other with Praise

1 Peter 3:9 tells us to "bless—that's your job, to bless. You'll be a blessing and also get a blessing."[26] The word blessing is rooted in the idea of celebrating with praise. Think of how celebrating your spouse with praise will bless you both. It is not hard to brag about him or her since there are so many things you can applaud. Find something to celebrate and say it face to face. You will be amazed how much it will change your feelings about each other.

Stop the Sarcasm

Peter also wrote, "Summing up: Be agreeable, be sympathetic, be loving, be compassionate, be humble. That goes for all of you, no exceptions. No retaliation. No sharp-tongued sarcasm."[27] I love sarcasm. It is my friend when talking to another man. But using sarcasm when talking to my wife is just plain dumb. She does not like it. Few women do when it comes to personal relation-

26 1 Peter 3:9, MES

27 1 Peter 3:8

ships. I have male friends that I can greet with, "What's up, ugly dog?" They laugh and say, "Nothing, buffalo breath." If I ever said anything like that to my wife – even in jest – I would be *under* the doghouse. Most of the time, however, when we use sarcasm with our spouse it is not in jest but is meant to hurt. That is sinful, and it always bites us back.

Be Kind

The Apostle Paul told us repeatedly, "Be kind to each other..."[28] That is one of the simplest commands in the Bible. Just be kind. When we practice kindness, we are humane and gracious. We are loving and respectful. I believe that if we obeyed that one simple command, it would cut the divorce rate drastically. I can't overemphasize how important this is. Just be nice. Your spouse is dying for you just to be kind. Men and women both respond positively to kind words and actions. It is a game-changer.

Kill the Cold Shoulder

I believe Paul gave great marriage counseling when he wrote, "Don't go to bed angry."[29] It is amazing to me how many couples give each other the silent treatment and go to the bedroom angry. I heard about one Christian couple that promised they would not go to bed while they were mad at each other. They had a lot of sleepless

28 Ephesians 4:32, ESV
29 Ephesians 4:26, MES

nights their first year of marriage. Kill the cold shoulder and talk to each other. Resolve conflict now! It will save your marriage.

I have read that men speak approximately 7,000 - 15,000 words per day and women say about 20,000 - 25,000 words per day.[30] Ladies, perhaps when you see your husband after work it is not that he doesn't want to talk, he just ran out of words for the day! Maybe that is why some old married men don't speak much. They only have a few words left, and they are not going to waste one.

It is important for a wife not to get frustrated with her husband if he does not talk as much as she does. That is certainly not unusual and, unless the lines of communication remain closed for extended periods of time, it is not a cause for concern. Just make sure you understand your husband's rhythms. Some people need to relax for a few minutes after work before they get into a deep conversation. Timing is critical for your husband to communicate meaningfully to you.

Men, it is also important to remember that your wife needs meaningful conversation. You may not need to talk as much, but she does. Part of loving your wife like Christ loves the church is being willing to make whatever effort is necessary to show and express love.

30 Catherine Griffin, *Science World Report* 2/20/2013.

Learn the Power of Respect

Husbands and wives often receive love differently. Most men receive love through feeling respected. I know that I do not have a deep need to hear the words "I love you" all the time. I certainly like those words, but they are not nearly as important to me as feeling respected by Kim. In Ephesians 5:33 Paul told men to *love their wives* and women to *respect their husbands*. Should men respect their wives and wives love their husbands? Of course. That just shows two different ways that husbands and wives feel and respond to love.

Whenever a spouse says things like "you always...," or "you never...," it shows a misunderstanding of this principle. Be careful not to tear your spouse down either privately or publically. It will damage your ability to communicate in a loving manner. Make sure that you discover what makes your spouse feel respected and pour out that respect generously.

Communicate Clearly

It is important for you to be direct and clear with each other. Husbands probably do not get hints as easily as wives. What may seem clear to a woman in a conversation may be completely lost on a man. If you want to spend more time with him tell him, "I want to spend more time with you." Don't tell him about how cool it was that your neighbors went on a two-week cruise together. He will start thinking about how awesome the food is on cruises and then make himself a sandwich. If you want him to take out the trash, tell him, "Honey, please take out the trash...now." When you say things like, "I wish somebody would take out the trash," he agrees with you. He wishes somebody would.

Nix the Nagging

1 Peter 3 teaches women who are trying to reach their husbands to "communicate without any words."[31] That does not mean use sign language. It implies that men do not respond to nagging. Many women make the mistake of believing that if they keep talking they will eventually wear their husband down and get him to do what he needs to do. That does not work. I have never known a man who was, "nagged to Jesus," and I have never seen a man who responds positively to carping and acrimony. He may eventually relent, but he will resent it.

Use Healing Words

Solomon tells us, "Irresponsible talk makes a real mess of things, but a reliable reporter is a healing presence."[32] The wisest man who ever lived teaches us that loose talk makes a mess of our relationships. I believe this is true in marriage, with your children, with your friends, and with your work. If you do not guard the things you say and how you say them, then it throws a potential grenade in the middle of all my environments.

31 1 Peter 3:1

32 Proverbs 13:17

Irresponsible talk comes in several forms.

- **Gossip**

Few things are more reckless than gossip. You can try to couch it in "concern," but gossip destroys relationships. Gossip is rooted in pride and insecurity and is the total opposite of love. People often gossip because they want to hear salacious details about someone else. Sometimes they gossip because they want to feel better about themselves or more superior than others. Most of the time gossip is designed to hurt the other person. Couples should avoid participating in this kind of sinful chatter. It destroys lives and will eventually harm your marriage.

- **Hurtful words**

Often, we speak words that are meant to cut and hurt. Sometimes this comes out of a bitter spirit and other times it comes from hurts and hang-ups from our past. Sometimes sarcasm can be skillfully used between people in a helpful or humorous way. Most of the time, however, it is simply meant to hurt. The Bible tells us that our words should build each other up.

- **Words spoken in anger**

Many times, we hurt the people closest to us by bursting out in anger. Guard your heart and your words so that you do not lose control and damage those you love. Something said in anger can be forgiven, but it takes a long time for that wound to heal.

- **Lying**

Lying is perhaps the most irresponsible of all the words we speak. The Bible says to speak the truth in love.

- **Unforgiving words**

We must always remember that no matter what happens to us, it is nothing compared to what we have done to God. Do not speak unforgiving words, but rather make it a habit to say some of the sweetest words ever spoken – "I forgive you."

Work on Your Communication Skills

Anything that gets neglected gets worse. This truth applies to your health, your finances, your business, and even trivial things like your golf game. It is particularly the case with your marriage. Don't be guilty of thinking that you never need to work on your relationship. Like everything else in life that is successful, a good marriage takes commitment. The essential requirement is your commitment to God. You are meant to be in a church together, to give together, and to serve together. Being involved together in regular worship, service, and small group community creates joy and marital stability. Do people who do these things ever have marriage problems? Yes, but only because there are no perfect marriages. But your life can be grace-centered.

King Solomon wrote, "It takes wisdom to have a good family, and it takes understanding to make it strong."[33] God will empower you with the wisdom and strength to build a healthy family when you depend on His grace. I believe God's grace is the greatest power in and for your marriage. It can heal the broken and restore the hurting. His grace transforms our communication and makes our marriage stronger.

33 Proverbs 24:3, NCV

Talk with Your Wife

1. *Tell your wife how thankful you are for her. Let her respond with how thankful she is for you.*
2. *Talk about sarcasm. Ask your wife if you have been sarcastic in a way that causes her to get upset. If you have been sarcastic in a hurtful way, ask her to forgive you.*
3. *Ask your wife what makes her feel valued. Tell her how you feel valued.*
4. *Talk about your social media use. Should you be more responsible with your posts? Do you spend too much time and energy on social media? Agree to work together to reflect your relationship with Christ on social media.*
5. *Pray out loud for each other. Ask God to draw your hearts closer to Him and each other.*

DAY NINE

Grace-Centered Words Will Change Your Marriage

When I was seven years old, my family moved from Elkin, North Carolina to Spartanburg, South Carolina. My dad got transferred with his job, and we lived there for two-and-a-half years before we moved back to North Carolina. My mom, being the good mom she is, did everything in her power to help me meet new friends. We were there less than a week when she signed me up for a local Little League baseball team.

To say I was nervous on the first day of practice would be an understatement. The field was beautiful and smelled of freshly cut grass. The sky was so blue that it hurt your eyes to look at it. It was pristine. However, I was a total stranger surrounded by boys I had never met and coaches that had a pernicious glimmer in their eye. It did not help that I had never played baseball before and they had already been practicing for two weeks.

When I met the coach, he just grunted. It was the kind of unspoken communication between a man and a boy that says, "I'm going to see what you are made of, grasshopper." He immediately put me at home plate to see if I could hit the ball. No introduction. No how-do-you-do. No good luck wishes. He spat a stream of tobacco juice and mumbled, "Let's see what this one's got." All activity stopped, and everyone stared at me while I walked the walk of shame to the batter's box.

When I saw the pitcher, my first thought was, "Nice beard." He was supposed to be ten years old, but if he was, the mad scientist who genetically engineered him lost his birth certificate. The team name was the Giants. I thought that was supposed to be a mascot, not a characterization of the players. The colossus managed a muscled sneer, and then fired a pitch past me like a missile. It came up and in on me so I flinched a little. The word "little" may understate my reaction a bit. I hit the dirt like a sniper shot me. It was way too close. His beard probably got in his eyes.

I will never forget what the coach said next. His eyes bulged, and brown tobacco spittle sprayed as he bellowed, "If he flinches again, hit him!" Hit him? Seriously? I was only seven. My life flashed before my eyes. Granted, it did not take very long, but it was long enough for me to conclude that I did not want to get maimed by a genetic freak.

I never played baseball again.

Would my life have been better if I played Little League baseball? I doubt it. At that point in my life, I was more interested in climbing trees than getting disfigured by a science experiment. Would I have been able to play in the Major Leagues and earn millions of dollars in front of adoring fans? Maybe. And then again, maybe a unicorn will show up at my house tonight with a pot of gold.

I don't believe in participation trophies or passing the buck. My point is that your words have power. They can build up, inspire, and give confidence or they can tear down, cause fear, and crush someone's dreams. Your words are like tools to shape and give hope or like weapons that can destroy.

As a spouse, your words matter. What you say is more important than what anyone else says. Choose your words wisely. They matter to your family and to God. Remember God's love to you through Jesus and let your words flow from there. You'll be amazed at the difference in your attitude and at the way your spouse responds.

Talk with Your Wife

1. *Share with your wife something God has been speaking to you about recently.*
2. *Ask your wife what God has been saying to her.*
3. *Take a moment and talk about how thankful you are for God's grace.*
4. *If you have children or plan to have children, talk about your goals in how you communicate with them.*
5. *Pray together and ask God to empower your words with His grace today.*

PART THREE

The Naked Truth about Success at Home and Work

In 1519 Hernàn Cortes and 600 men landed on the shore of Mexico armed with the mission to conquer the Aztec Empire. Attempting to inspire his men to believe that victory was the only option, he burned the ships. Some historians debate whether he burned them, but most historians agree that he purposely destroyed them so that retreat was not an option.

I once saw a pizza advertisement that claimed to offer thousands of possible combinations. I don't know if that is a good strategy for selling pizza, but I do know that it is a terrible strategy for being successful in balancing work and marriage. If you leave your options open, then you will become discontented. Dissatisfaction slyly creeps into the undisciplined heart. When that happens, God's purpose for your marriage and work become vulnerable. Divorce becomes an unstated option. You leave your heart open for a crisis of confidence about your work and your purpose in life. You will face the temptation to disengage, which will lead to discouragement.

You must burn the ships. Take all options off the table other than a total commitment to God, your family, and pursuing with passion God's purpose in your work. Maintain your focus, and you will be happy and blessed at home and your job.

DAY TEN

Succeeding at Work Without Failing at Home

God designed work to be a beautiful expression of worship through our gifts and creativity. But humans sinned, and God put a curse on the earth. He told Adam that his work would change. What began as a blessing became cursed with toil, labor, and frustration. However, when a person follows Christ, God redeems his or her life and purpose. That includes your work and home life. While you can't have a perfect home or job here on earth, you can have a redeemed work life and family life that fulfills God's purpose.

Let's look at what God declared about work and home life in the creation story.

> Then God said, "Let us make man in our image, after our likeness. And let them have dominion over the fish of the sea and over the birds of the heavens and over the livestock and over all the earth and over every creeping thing that creeps on the earth." So God created man in his own image, in the image of God he created him; male and female he created them. And God blessed them. And God said to them, "Be fruitful and multiply and fill the earth and subdue it, and have dominion over the fish of the sea and over the birds of the heavens and over every living thing that moves on the earth." And God said, "Behold, I have given you every plant yielding seed that is on the face of all the earth, and every tree with seed in its fruit. You shall have them for food. And to every beast of the earth and

> to every bird of the heavens and to everything that creeps on the earth, everything that has the breath of life, I have given every green plant for food." And it was so. And God saw everything that he had made, and behold, it was very good. And there was evening and there was morning, the sixth day.[34]

Work Must be God-Focused

Since God made us in His image, we must reflect His character and purpose. He blessed work, and we are called to represent Him in and through our work. Work was never intended to be a burden but rather a blessing.

Elsewhere in scripture, God told us not to worship false images. Any form of idolatry is forbidden because God loves us. He knows that when we worship anything other than Him, it eventually destroys us. Our work is not to be an idol, but we are to worship God through our work. Seeing work as worship helps keep you from worshipping your job. When you value your livelihood as your source, you will begin to put it first in your life. Work is important, of course, but God never intended for you to work so much that you neglect your family or your health.

Adam and Eve began with God's blessings. He blessed their work, their creativity, their authority, and their home life. Labor and home life were blessed because God designed everything to find its purpose in Him. When we

34 Genesis 1:26-31, ESV

begin with God as our source, the natural response is worship.

Once you begin to see your work as worship, then you can recognize that it has eternal significance. I love how the Apostle Paul captured the essence of this doctrine.

> So here's what I want you to do, God helping you: Take your everyday, ordinary life—your sleeping, eating, going-to-work, and walking-around life—and place it before God as an offering. Embracing what God does for you is the best thing you can do for him. Don't become so well-adjusted to your culture that you fit into it without even thinking. Instead, fix your attention on God. You'll be changed from the inside out. Readily recognize what he wants from you, and quickly respond to it. Unlike the culture around you, always dragging you down to its level of immaturity, God brings the best out of you, develops well-formed maturity in you.[35]

When my work is God-focused, then I can live for his purpose even if I work with challenging people or don't particularly enjoy my job.

Work Must be Grace-Focused

God intended for us to live our lives immersed in His grace from the very beginning. God gives us His grace because

35 Romans 12:1-2, MES

of His love and character. We do not earn it. He freely gives us His unearned, undeserved, unmerited kindness and favor. His favor had filled creation from the beginning. They did nothing to earn it. God blessed their life and work because that is what God does. That was His plan from the beginning.

God said, "Let us *make* man..." "Make" is the same word used in Exodus 23:22 when God promised to do the work necessary to make a covenant with Israel and provide a Savior. Jesus fulfilled this promise through His finished work on the cross. It is all about His grace!

Our work must focus on God's grace. It was so from the very beginning. Through His grace, we find the ability to create and the capacity to worship and glorify God through our work. God empowers us to *rule over* our work, rather than be *dominated by* it.

You Must be King over Your Work

From the beginning, God planned for you to rule over the created order, not for your job to dominate you. He told humans to subdue the earth and have dominion over creation. That means God wants us to reign in our world and work. He plans for us to conquer it and bring it into subjection. We are to exercise the authority Christ has given us. God has given you the capacity to bring your work under subjection through the power of Christ. We are free to do our best, to improve, and to rule over what we do for a living. We are not to let our job rule us, but we are to reign over it. It must serve us.

God also commanded that we be fruitful. We are to grow, increase, multiply, and create abundantly for his glory. We must trust God for the increase in finances and skill. God wants to bless your work, but we must trust in His provision.

In the end, God looked at all He created and declared that it was "very good." Everything He spoke into existence was fruitful, lovely, delightful, joyous, and righteous. When we keep work in its proper place, then we can experience the blessings God declared over it.

Talk with Your Wife

1. *How can husbands and wives see work as worship?*
2. *Ask your wife if she feels that you spend too much time at work. Talk about your finances and what your financial goals are and how you can work together to reach them.*
3. *Talk about God's grace with your wife. How does His unearned, unmerited, undeserved favor impact your view of your job? Can you depend on God's grace for success at work?*
4. *Talk with your wife about balance. What do you think makes a proper balance? What does she think?*
5. *Pray with your wife about your job – both yours and hers. Pray that God empowers you to see work as worship and to depend on His grace for success.*

DAY ELEVEN

Resting for Success

Kim and I started Avalon Church in 2001. We had no money, no members, and no place to meet. For the first two years, we met in four different locations because we got kicked out of every place we met. We told people they could worship with us if they could find us. Wouldn't it be great if all pastors were so filled with faith that they never stressed or worried? I worried about money, organization, facilities, management, staffing, community relations, what people thought of me, and probably the same kind of stresses that you worry about with your job. On top of that, I had to prepare a sermon every week.

One day, about eighteen months after we started the church, I had a breakdown. While driving on the Interstate, I began to weep uncontrollably. I could not even see, so I pulled over and cried for a long time. I told God, "I can't do this." That was a turning point in my life with my family and work. Did my struggles completely end that day? No, I occasionally failed to rest in God. But thankfully, I began practicing what the Bible teaches about giving my burdens to God. It was the beginning of a journey that brought peace in my work and at home. We all must walk that path daily.

Rest Rather than Worry

Jesus taught us how to depend on Him for our daily work. I believe this kind of faith is the key to living a balanced life. Resting in God for success changes the way you work and brings balance to your life.

> "Therefore I tell you, do not be anxious about your life, what you will eat or what you will drink, nor about your body, what you will put on. Is not life more than food, and the body more than clothing? Look at the birds of the air: they neither sow nor reap nor gather into barns, and yet your heavenly Father feeds them. Are you not of more value than they? And which of you by being anxious can add a single hour to his span of life? And why are you anxious about clothing? Consider the lilies of the field, how they grow: they neither toil nor spin, yet I tell you, even Solomon in all his glory was not arrayed like one of these. But if God so clothes the grass of the field, which today is alive and tomorrow is thrown into the oven, will he not much more clothe you, O you of little faith? Therefore do not be anxious, saying, 'What shall we eat?' or 'What shall we drink?' or 'What shall we wear?' For the Gentiles seek after all these things, and your heavenly Father knows that you need them all. But seek first the kingdom of God and his righteousness, and all these things will be added to you."[36]

Change Your Perspective

Jesus told us not to be anxious, uneasy or nervous. Don't worry about food, clothing, or shelter – all related to our work and life in general. That is easier said than done. You can know in your head that Jesus provides for every

36 Matthew 6:25-33, ESV

part of life, but it is sometimes difficult to practice that kind of rest.

Shifting your perspective is fundamentally an exercise in faith. You must believe that God is the source, not you, not your strength, not your talent, and not your work ethic. When you realize that you are not the most important part of the equation, then it frees you to trust in God and rest in Him. God is the source of your success. He is the source of your supply. Your job is to be faithful and trust in Him.

Set Right Priorities

Jesus promised that if we seek God's kingdom first, then He will supply all the success we need. He is not saying that work is unimportant, but that our primary focus is to be on God's grace and provision. Seeking His kingdom means seeking God's agenda first. It means that the gospel must be our primary focus. We are to trust His sovereignty, Christ's authority, and to seek the blessings that flow from Christ. God's kingdom is fleshed out through the church. It is impossible to put God's kingdom first apart from participating in, serving through, giving to, and living in community with a local body of believers.

To seek His kingdom first means that my priorities at work shift from me to God. Am I under His authority? Am I seeking His blessings? Am I using my gifts at work for His glory and His kingdom? Focusing on God changes how you work and how you see your employment. It empowers you to love, to gain freedom from stress, and to rest in His power.

Embrace Grace for Success

Jesus said we are to seek His righteousness first. In other words, we must put the gospel and God's grace at the center of all we do at work. Since we can't become righteous by good deeds, then we must also seek His grace at work. God's undeserved, unearned, unmerited favor is the key to salvation, but it is also the key to success at work!

Embracing God's grace leads to a fundamental shift in our thinking. Using the gifts, talents, and abilities that God gave you is a spiritual exercise. Your job should be a place that you use these gifts to bring glory to God and grow spiritually. Your job should be a place of worship, a mission field, and a ministry. You can grow spiritually through the pressures, people, and problems in your job.

Work that aligns with God's purpose for your life is fulfilling and fruitful. When you connect your faith with your job and let God lead your career, you start to realize that your daily labors have eternal significance. You can stop feeling frustrated and fatigued by your job and start seeing your work from God's perspective!

Take A Sabbath

God gave the gift of Sabbath to help us avoid the feelings of burnout, exhaustion, and loss of passion. Although we are no longer under Old Testament Law, I believe that the principle of taking regular rest is life-changing.

In Exodus 31:12-18 God repeated instructions for the Nation of Israel to observe Sabbath rest every week. Verse seventeen tells us that God created the heavens and earth in six days and rested on the seventh day. It also says God's rest resulted in refreshment. God is all-powerful and therefore cannot get weary, so why does it state that He became refreshed? Why did God need rejuvenating and replenishing rest? The Hebrew root word that is translated "refreshed" means "to take breath"[37]." We would say it like this, "I want to catch my breath." *Breathing in* was the opposite of what God did for six days. He *breathed out* when he created. He *breathed in* when he rested. Since God needs no rest, the reason He did this was to instruct us on how to live our lives.

When we work, we are creating. We are "breathing out." When we take a Sabbath rest, we are "breathing in" or catching our breath. I think the principle here is incredibly powerful. One day a week we should rest, recover, rebuild, re-energize, and breathe in.

37 Strong's Hebrew Concordance, #5314

Talk with Your Wife

1. *What are you worried about at work?*
2. *How can you rest in God's grace for success at work?*
3. *Talk about your priorities as a family. Do you both agree on what the priorities should be?*
4. *Do you both rest enough and take regular days off? How can you support and encourage each other in this pursuit?*
5. *Pray together about resting in God's grace for your needs at work and home. Make a commitment to pursue this together.*

DAY TWELVE

Get Better at Your Job

Matthew 25:14-30 records the Parable of the Talents. The gist of the story is that a wealthy and powerful businessman went on a journey. Before he left, he gave each of his servants some of his money with the expectation that each one would manage the money and make a profit. To one man he gave five talents. To another, he gave two talents. To the other, he gave one talent. Each servant had differing abilities, but each had the same responsibility - manage what the boss gave him in a way that pleased the boss. By the way, a talent was worth approximately 1.2 million dollars.

Upon his return, the boss brought each servant in to give an accounting of what he had done with his money. The servants that received five and two talents respectively doubled their boss's money. The boss rewarded them both. The servant that received one talent wasted his time and opportunity and returned no profit for his boss. His lord took the talent and judged him for his laziness. He even called the worker wicked.

We learn many principles from this story. I believe the talents represent our lives, our time, our abilities, our money, and our work. These are God's, not ours. God expects us to leverage them for His glory and purpose. They have great value. The way we view God exceedingly affects the way we live. But perhaps the most important principle is that God expects us to invest our life for His glory. A wasted life leads to sin, regret, and loss.

Integrity Matters

The Old Testament account of the life of Joseph is one of my favorite stories in the Bible. Joseph handled a difficult situation with unquestioned character. He had been sold into slavery by his brothers and was now working for an Egyptian officer named Potiphar. Potiphar's wife tried her best to lure Joseph into having an affair with her, but he refused. His refusal landed him in prison because she lied about him when he refused her advances and claimed that he tried to rape her. But despite his circumstances, he maintained a positive attitude and lived with honor. He faced an integrity crisis but trusted God for the outcome.

Sometimes we are tempted to think that God has abandoned us in tough times. We get lured into discarding our principles and integrity. But God is always with us and always shows us His faithful love when we trust Him. In the end, God delivered Joseph, exalted him to a position of honor, and used him to save the lives of millions of people in Egypt and the surrounding areas. God always has a plan to use us even when we feel like He has put us in an impossible situation.

Integrity is critical to your success at work. You may be able to gain a short-term advantage by dishonesty or cheating, but character always underpins long-term success. Losing your core principles leads to a loss of moral authority and will eventually doom your career and negatively impact your personal life. Integrity matters when investing your life rather than wasting it.

Go the Extra Mile

Abraham gave his servant the task of finding a wife for his son Isaac. As he went to Abraham's homeland to fulfill his duty, he prayed that God would reveal to him the right woman - one who would do something rather extraordinary. When he asked for water, she would offer to water his ten camels as well. That may not sound very unusual, but camels can drink up to 50 gallons at a time.

The first woman he met was named Rebekah. Sure enough, she offered to water his camels when he asked for a drink. Think about that task. She most likely drew around 500 gallons of water with a jug that held five gallons or less. She may have had to fill the container as many as 100 times! She went the extra mile. She did more than was expected. She went above and beyond. She did not complain or say that it was not her job to water the camels.

Going the extra mile changes your career. When you do more than is expected, you position yourself for a blessing. Many people want to do the bare minimum. Doing the bare minimum is not enough to achieve success. Fruitful people do more than others. They work hard. They show up early. They stay late, if necessary. They have a positive attitude and serve those above and below them on the organizational chart. Living with this kind of attitude positions you to advance at work, to receive promotions and commendations, to receive better pay, and to become an indispensable employee. When you go the extra mile, you gain a good reputation and position yourself to honor Christ and represent Him at work.

Talk with Your Wife

1. *How can you protect your moral integrity at work? If you lie on a report, lie to your boss, fudge an expense report, steal from the office, or misrepresent a product to make a sale, how does it impact your integrity?*
2. *Does it seem like those who cut corners at your work get ahead? How can you trust God for the outcome even if it seems like doing the right thing will lead to failure?*
3. *How can you guard your relational integrity at work? What should your policy be about having lunch alone with a person of the opposite sex?*
4. *How can you go above and beyond at your job? How can this help people see Jesus in your life?*
5. *Pray for God to bless and advance both of you - husband and wife - at work and to help you invest your lives for God's purpose.*

DAY THIRTEEN

Finding Joy in Your Work

See if this sounds familiar. The same old alarm clock rings at the same old time. You get out of the same old bed, brush the same old teeth, climb into the same old shower, go into the same old kitchen, and drink the same old coffee. You slide into the same old car, drive the same old road to the same old job, work with the same old people, and get off at the same old time. You drive the same old way back to the same old house. After supper, you flop into the same old chair and fall asleep watching the same old TV. You wake up and go to the same old bed, ask the same old wife the same old question, get the same old answer, and start it all over again the next morning. If this is you, then perhaps you need to rediscover the joy in your work.

The Apostle Paul wrote a letter to a group of believers in a church that he started in the ancient city of Ephesus. They were real people with real problems just like we have today. They had problems with their boss, their work relationships, their money, and their family. I love how The Message paraphrase captures the essence of finding joy in your job in Ephesians 6:7. It states, "And work with a smile on your face, always keeping in mind that no matter who happens to be giving the orders, you're really serving God."

Work with a smile on your face. Have a good attitude. Remember that you are really working for God at the job He has provided. Be thankful for His provision. You can deal with difficulties when you remember that you work for God. Even if you don't love your job, do it for the love of God, the love of your family, and the love of those God has put in your path. In doing so you will transform your attitude about work and will begin to discover and work with joy.

Do you remember the miraculous story of Daniel and the den of lions? It is one of my favorites. Deliverance from lions captures only a small part of the story. God recorded for us that Daniel had "an excellent spirit." He had a good attitude despite terrible circumstances. Think about the challenges he faced. He was kidnapped and forced into serving the king who conquered his homeland. That King ripped him away from his family and forced him to live in a place that was hostile to his religion and his heritage. If he did his job well, then it helped strengthen the very regime that terrorized him. If he did not do his job well, then he would be put to death. And to make matters worse, he was most likely castrated, a practice that was widely used in the ancient world to keep conquered people from reproducing and rebelling against the kingdom. Although the Bible does not cite his castration, Daniel served under the authority of the prince of the eunuchs. All eunuchs got castrated. If anyone ever had a reason to have a bad attitude about a job, it was Daniel.

Think about how difficult Daniel's working conditions were. He was a member of the royal family in Judah before he got captured. His captors forced him to serve the conquering, heathen king. Eventually, he served eight different kings during his time in Babylon, although only four get mentioned in the Book of Daniel. He served the

Babylonian Empire and then the Persian Empire for approximately 70 years. But even with great opposition, he always came out on top. When kings and political leaders set up a new government, they rarely kept the old guard. But Daniel rose to prominence and maintained his position under eight different kings and two entirely different empires. Unusual indeed! But it demonstrates God's sovereignty, the power of faith, and the importance of a good attitude.

Your attitude is supremely significant. It reveals our trust in God and impacts the people around us. Although it is a well-worn cliché, it bears a powerful truth: your attitude determines your altitude. Your spirit and faith propel you. Negativity and bitterness weigh you down like a millstone around your neck. Your attitude is a choice. Like Daniel, you do not have to let your circumstances determine the way you react. You can choose to rise above your conditions and work with a smile on your face.

Talk with Your Wife

1. *What constitutes a good attitude? Do you think people see those qualities in you?*
2. *Do you ever display a bad attitude at home? How does your attitude affect your family?*
3. *Do you find joy in your work? How would reminding yourself that you work for God and His purpose help?*
4. *What can you do daily to improve your attitude?*
5. *Pray together and thank God for his blessings. Ask Him to help you possess the kind of attitude Daniel had.*

PART FOUR

The Naked Truth about Money

My first job after graduating from college was serving as a youth pastor at a church in Panama City, Florida. In my first year, we went on a snow skiing trip to Gatlinburg, Tennessee. We arrived at our destination with over fifty kids from Florida.

The next morning, we checked out our rentals and headed off to the slopes. I had to go to "ski school" because I did not know anything about skiing. The instructor told me the first thing I must learn was to fall correctly. I got an "A" in that part of the class. It was the staying up part that I failed.

Once the disaster of ski school was over, I hit the trails. I mean that in the literal sense of the word. Every ten feet I experienced a violent collision with the ground. Between inglorious falls, several boys from our youth group asked me to ski with them. They led me to the highest, most difficult slope at the resort.

Theoretically, when you get off the ski lift, you are supposed to lean forward, level your skis, and stand up. Theoretically. I got caught on the chairlift, dragged off the platform, and dangled between heaven and earth. Of course, the boys left me to ski down the mountain alone.

There were a couple of relevant things I did not know at the time. First, I did not know how to ski. Second, I was unaware that a Winter Special Olympics event was happening at the bottom of the slope I was skiing. What you don't know can harm you.

As I inadvertently headed for the greatest embarrassment of my life, my skills grew. I skied a few feet, fell for several yards, searched for my skis for a few minutes, took several minutes to fasten them, and then repeated this exhausting process.

On my final attempt to get down the hill, I managed to stay vertical. But any incremental improvements in verticality were offset by an acute increase in velocity. Mass times acceleration equals embarrassment squared. In other words, I went so fast that my tears met on the back of my head.

Just ahead I saw a roped off course with children participating in a race. There was a finish line with a tape that the winner got to break. It was a Special Olympics event. The kids were amazing. They beamed. Incredible parents and volunteers crowded around the finish line taking pictures, cheering, and celebrating. It was a beautiful moment.

I did not plan to enter the race. My mind screamed no, but my skis would not listen. I saw the finish line. I even saw the young man leading the race. I yelled for him to move out of the way. He probably could not hear me because of the crowd noise.

Do you believe in miracles? I do. When I knocked that kid over, I didn't fall. Miraculously I took the lead. The tape loomed. Cheering. Clapping. Filming. They yelled, "You can do it."

And I did. I won. The organizers tried to give me a medal. They rescinded the offer when they discovered I did not register.

I went to the mountain to learn to ski. Instead, I learned that what you don't know can hurt you. This principle is valid for winter sports and finances. If you don't know what the Bible teaches about blessed money, then you will hurt financially.

DAY FOURTEEN

The Power of Stewardship

If you are going to live a life that is blessed financially, you must discover if you are an owner or a manager. I am not talking about whether you own or rent, buy or lease. Let the financial experts debate that. I am asking, "Do you own your stuff or does God own it?" In God's opinion, He does. He says, "…The earth is the Lord's, and everything in it."[38] Jesus said, "So if you have not been trustworthy in handling worldly wealth, who will trust you with true riches? And if you have not been trustworthy with someone else's property, who will give you property of your own? No servant can serve two masters. Either he will hate the one and love the other, or he will be devoted to the one and despise the other. You cannot serve both God and Money."[39]

In these verses, God gives us a test. He uses our money to see how spiritually mature we are. He uses how you handle money and material possessions as the indicator of whether He can trust you with certain spiritual blessings. "Handling worldly wealth" means managing your money. If you are not wise in money management, why should God trust you with the real deal – spiritual wealth? In other words, how much God blesses you is, to a large degree, determined by the way you handle the material things in life. If you are not a faithful money manager, God says that you are not very responsible.

If God does not own your stuff, then your stuff owns you! Once again, I am not talking about owning versus

38 Psalm 24:1 (NLT)
39 Luke 16:11-13 (NIV)

renting. I believe in entrepreneurs and risk takers. It is not God's will for everyone to own a business, but many never know the power of ownership and increased wealth because they are afraid. The penetrating question is, do you recognize God as the owner of everything? When we acknowledge that God owns it all, then, He transforms us.

Stewardship Requires Honesty

King David wrote, "But you desire honesty from the heart, so you can teach me to be wise in my inmost being."[40] Get honest with yourself. Take a long, hard look in the mirror and get brutally honest. It is a lot easier to make excuses or blame someone or something else for our financial problems. But being honest is the first step toward blessed money.

Did you ever go to an amusement park that had a mirror that made you look tall and thin? It distorts reality. It is fun to imagine that you are taller or thinner. I like to imagine myself being seven feet tall, playing in the NBA, and dunking the basketball with a primal scream.

Isn't that the way we like to look at ourselves; with distorted reality? It is hard to look at yourself in the mirror of God's Word, but it is necessary. We must know our own heart before we can change. We should take an unbiased look at our financial picture before we can improve it.

40 Psalm 51:6, NLT

Consider what Job said, "If I have put my trust in money, if my happiness depends on wealth... it would mean that I denied the God of heaven."[41]

You must decide whether you want to live with God's blessings or if you want to live with stress and pressure all your life. Yes, you should have goals and motivation for success. However, I am not talking about having nice things, but about possessions owning you. Does your definition of success match up with God's? Are you living to acquire things you can't afford to impress people you don't even like? You can choose to get out of debt. You can live in peace. You can acquire real prosperity. But you can't have it if you live like most Americans – spend more than you make, live on credit cards, rack up bad debt, make minimum payments, live a lie, and have no clue where your money goes. Before you can live a blessed life, you must know your heart and get honest about your desires, goals, and motivations.

Stewardship Requires Knowing Your Weaknesses

We all have weaknesses when it comes to spending money. For some people, it is shoes. Some crave the latest golf clubs. The list is endless. My weakness is tools. I guess it is a man thing, but I just love tools. I don't even use all the ones I own, but it sure is fun to get new ones.

41 Job 31:24, 28, LB

A few years ago, I bought two leaf blowers. Not the wimpy electrical kind. These were gas guzzling devices capable of blowing paint off a car. They were identical, as in same brand, same horsepower, same model, same size, and same color. A man could justify having two blowers if he had a lawn service, a forest, or a yard the size of Rhode Island. He could even defend his purchase if one didn't operate properly. Both of mine worked just fine. I had one tree in my front yard that was ten feet tall at the time. It took about three minutes and forty-two seconds to blow off my driveway. Here is the kicker. I didn't even mow my yard. I had a close friend that did it for me at the "pastor's discount."

Why did I have two blowers? I did not defend against my weakness when I went to the store. I drool for tools. I justified spending that money because I did not obey biblical principles. What can you learn from my mistake?

1) **Choose contentment.** God says, "Be content with what you have..."[42] How many times could we save money or avoid debt if we would choose to be thankful for what we have? Contentment helps us avoid spending creep. If we do not discipline ourselves to remain contented, we will spend every penny of a raise, a windfall, or a tax return. Instead of saving, we'll buy a bigger house, trade in our car, get a bigger loan, or spend outside our plan.

42 Hebrews 13:5, NIV

2) **Seek satisfaction from the right things.** God says, "Why spend money on what does not satisfy?"[43] Have you ever made an impulse buy? It is a good policy to sleep on the decision before major purchases. Always make a list before shopping and stick with it. Buying things will never fill a void in your life. A new pair of expensive jeans, a new car, or a new shotgun will not make you any more loved than you are right now.
3) **Stick to a financial plan.** God says, "... stupid people spend their money as fast as they get it."[44] Ouch. People talk about the Bible being hard to understand. I don't think those people have read the Bible. It is not hard to comprehend, just real hard to obey, sometimes. We often disguise luxuries or wants as legitimate needs. Beware of this. I did not need another blower. I only wanted another one. Fortunately, my lack of discretion was a relatively minor purchase. When we fail to live by a financial plan, we set ourselves up for financial failure. Spending without a plan leads to mortgages we can barely pay, upside down car loans, excessive credit card debt, making minimum payments, and living under the stress of financial pressure. The good news is you can make a change as soon as you get honest with yourself and admit where you need help.

43 Isaiah 55:2

44 Proverbs 21:20, GNT

Talk with Your Wife

1. *Ask your wife if she thinks you both see God as the owner of everything in your life.*
2. *Talk about what this looks like practically. Do you bring the full tithe? Do you worry about money?*
3. *Get honest with each other about your financial picture. Do you save enough? Do you live by a budget?*
4. *Discuss your financial weaknesses and fears with each other.*
5. *Pray with your wife about your finances. Ask God to help you live with blessed money rather than cursed money.*

DAY FIFTEEN

God's Plan for Your Financial Success

God has a financial plan that will make you successful. The Bible teaches God-breathed principles that transcend all cultures and eras. His economic blueprint does not depend on how much money you make. Nevertheless, the burden is on you to make the decision to live by His principles or by your feelings. God's laws work no matter how high or low your income level is. His truths are transcendent.

Every person possesses unique abilities and passions. God, in His wisdom, has given us distinctive personalities, different levels of giftedness, and personal yearnings. God's plans work for every personality and gift type. Whether you are a business owner and desire to make enough money to travel the world, or you work for someone else, want to live a simple life, and plan to retire early, His principles work the same. Here are a few things He teaches us about our relationship with money.

Put God First

Put first things first. The principle of prioritizing must come first. Isn't that wonderfully redundant? Why am I stating the obvious repeatedly? Most people struggle to give priority to the important stuff!

God says that He MUST be first. *He* is the priority in our finances. How do I put Him first? God says the first step is tithing. "The purpose of tithing is to teach you always to put God first in your lives."[45]

The Bible teaches us that the tithe is the first ten percent of our income. Notice it is the first part, not the leftovers. God has always demanded to be first in every part of our life. Once I prioritize God in my finances, it is easier to begin to prioritize other aspects of my spending.

Pay Yourself Second

God wants you to save and invest in yourself. Wise people do not live at or above their means, but they keep some margin in their lives. King Solomon wrote, "The wise man saves for the future, but the foolish man spends whatever he gets."[46] It is tempting to be short-sighted and to trick ourselves into thinking that we can spend every penny we make on our immediate needs and desires. The truth is, however, that there will always be unexpected costs and emergencies. That is not God's punishment; it is just life. Life happens. Cars wear out, washing machines break down, houses need repair, children get sick, and unexpected things happen. I need a plan for emergencies and retirement, or I will constantly live in a state of panic and drama.

45 Deuteronomy 14:23, LB

46 Proverbs 21:20

Cultivate Contentment

Be thankful. It sounds simple, but it works. Be thankful for what you have. Learn to be content, and it will quell lots of unnecessary spending and unwanted debt. How many times do we buy something that just hangs in the closet or gathers dust in our basement? Thankfulness and contentment simplify your life and bring a margin to your finances. The Apostle Paul said, "For I have learned to be satisfied with what I have."[47]

Follow A Budget

I will give more detail about budgeting in the next chapter, but wise spending takes a written plan. If you do not have a written plan, then you do not have a plan. Most of us experience cash leakage – money that we don't remember spending – because we do not have a way of tracking or managing our expenditures. Writing out your plan and following a budget works. When my wife, Kim, and I wrote our financial goals on paper, started following a written budget, and began tracking our spending, we were amazed at how much money we saved each month.

Enjoy Life

God wants you to enjoy life. Some feel guilty about this and don't enjoy God's blessings. Others miss out on real joy because they seek it in the wrong things. God desires to bless you! Following His plan opens the possibility of

47 Philippians 4:11, GNT

fully enjoying our time here. Jesus said He came to give us life to the fullest.

I do not believe God ever gives us commands that are harmful or burdensome. They are always for our good. Sometimes they may seem weighty, but when we begin to practice them by faith, we learn that God wants to bless us.

King Solomon was a wise man. The Bible says that he was the wisest man who ever lived. When he wrote the book of Ecclesiastes, he wrote from the perspective of one that did not live for God's purposes. That is why the book has such a depressing theme about the meaninglessness of life. However, even in his depressed state, he observed that God's ways are always the best ways. Consider his thoughts on money and work. "And it is a good thing to receive wealth from God and the good health to enjoy it. To enjoy your work and accept your lot in life—that is indeed a gift from God."[48]

Life is indeed a gift from God. Enjoy it!

48 Ecclesiastes 5:19, NLT

Talk with Your Wife

1. *Do you believe that you are putting God first in your finances as a family?*
2. *Do you think you are saving enough for retirement or for current purchases?*
3. *How can you both be content with what God has given you? What are your goals? How can you reach them?*
4. *Are you enjoying life? Often, we live under stress because we are envious or discontented with life. How can you enjoy the simple things of life more?*
5. *Pray together and ask God to help you live by His financial principles.*

DAY SIXTEEN

Building a Financial Blueprint

Knowledge is the accumulation of facts. Wisdom consists of knowing how to apply knowledge. Knowledge means knowing *what*. Wisdom means knowing *why* and *how*. I can possess abundant knowledge, but if I do not have the wisdom to apply it, then it does me no good.

When my children were toddlers, I warned them not to touch hot things like stoves or heaters. They had sufficient information about the dangers of hot objects. The experience of feeling something that burned them, however, gave them the wisdom not to touch items that could harm them.

You can have knowledge without wisdom. People get burned all the time even though they have good information. Most people know that they should not spend more than they make. You do not have to have a degree in economics to grasp intuitive financial concepts. Instinctive understanding does not keep people from spending too much. What is their problem? They have knowledge but no wisdom. Wisdom comes from God. Solomon understood this notion when he wrote, "For the Lord grants wisdom! From his mouth come knowledge and understanding. He grants a treasure of good sense to the godly. He is their shield, protecting those who walk with integrity."[49]

49 Proverbs 2:6-7

Budgets Build Wisdom

Some perceive a spending plan in the same way they approach an annual physical; necessary but uncomfortable. Perhaps a better image is warm rolls. They are good for you, and after you have had one, you are glad that you did. I have found that operating within a budget leads to more fun and freedom. I know my money is going to be there and I don't stand around scratching my head wondering where it went. You are thinking about having a hot, buttered roll, aren't you?

Budgeting is nothing more than a common-sense approach to handling money. My wife, Kim, has a way of making food last. We budget how much money gets spent on groceries each month, and she is a master at stretching a dollar and making everybody in our house happy. She is great at dividing stuff up into portions. She will even hide things so that we do not run out. I laugh at her sometimes, but I'm always thankful we have plenty of good food to eat.

I look at a budget like a bag of chips. When our children were younger, Kim made our family portion out chips by eating them from plates. She didn't want anyone to eat out of the bag. That is like having a budget. Everybody gets fed, and the chips last longer. Having no budget is like eating right out of the bag. Everybody just grabs them until they are gone. Chips get wasted. Everybody argues about who ate the most chips. Budgets are the only practical way to get a grip on your bag of chips.

Creating a budget usually requires three steps. The first step is confirming your spending. Without a budget, you have no idea what you are spending or where your money goes. I challenge you to take a month and write down everything you spend – I mean everything. It will probably shock you how much you spend on eating out, entertainment, late fees, and unplanned expenditures. You can't get financially healthy until you get an accurate measurement of what you spend.

After identifying your spending habits, you must *analyze your spending*. What things can you forgo? How can you cut back and still get what you need? A good example for most people is how much they spend on food. You must eat, but do you have to pay as much for food as you do now? Eating at home, though not as convenient, is ordinarily much less expensive than eating out. What about your phone service? Is there a better plan that will save you money? Do you need a cell phone AND a home phone? What about your television service? Could you do without it? Do you watch all the channels? Could you get a cheaper package and still enjoy what you watch most? Could you ditch the television plan and use an online service? What about the Internet? Could you save on your power bill by turning off lights or going to more energy efficient lights? Could you lower your heating bill by lowering the thermostat? These may seem like small steps, but they could add up to savings of potentially thousands of dollars per year.

Once you have identified your spending habits, you should manage your spending. That is where the budgeting process starts to help you. Find something that works for you. Kim and I do much better by having separate bank accounts. We budget how much money gets put into each account. We budget our tithe, food, entertainment, clothing, dry-cleaning, vacation, savings, house expenses, and every penny we spend. After lots of trial and error (and lots of arguments) we discovered that we work better with a joint account to pay most of our bills, a savings account, and two separate personal accounts. We put the budgeted amount in each account at the beginning and middle of each month. Then we leave each other alone. I do not manage her account, and she does not control mine. It also keeps us from having to be so detailed. If we can save money, then we get to keep it and do what we want with it. It is a system that works for us.

Talk with Your Wife

1. *Discuss your budget. Do you have one? Do you need to get help setting a budget?*
2. *When is the last time you argued over money? What do you think is the cause of that argument?*
3. *What can you do to support each other in how you deal with money? What do you need from each other?*
4. *What are some ways you could save money and still get what you need?*
5. *Pray that God gives you a spirit of wisdom in your finances.*

DAY SEVENTEEN

Stop Dreaming and Start Doing

King Solomon said, "Dreaming instead of doing is foolishness."[50]

Most of us dream of having plenty of money. We've all fantasized about what we would do with an enormous windfall. Solomon, one of the wisest, wealthiest men ever to live, told us to stop daydreaming and start doing. In other words, create a game plan. When you follow a game plan, you win. When you stop following your game plan, you lose.

When I was twenty-seven years old, I coached the men's basketball team at my alma mater. None of the athletes were on scholarship, so they played for the love of the sport. Our athletic budget was an insult to athletic budgets. As a result, our travel, meal stipends, and accommodations typically rated less than five stars. I had a blast.

One of our away games was at the home court of an archrival. We had won on our home court and at neutral sites before, but we had never tasted victory on their campus. Not ever. At this game, thousands of students filled the stands. The noise was deafening. It was a great atmosphere for a college game. And as usual, we were losing.

We fell behind by seventeen points in the second half. It looked like another defeat at their place. Being a first-year head coach, I was nervous and frustrated. I called a time-out and started yelling at the players -- the ones on

50 Ecclesiastes 5:7, LB

our team, not the other guys. I kept saying that we had to start following the game plan. I said it over and over, mainly because I did not know what else to say.

Then a weird thing happened. Our team started executing the game plan and doing what we had practiced. I was surprised because my guys never listened before. We slowly clawed our way back into the game. The deficit was seventeen points. Then it was ten points...five points... two points. I was ecstatic! Only six seconds remained in the game and we were down by two points. One of our players fouled a 6'10" giant from their team. Thousands screamed. My palms sweated. As the human mountain prepared to shoot two free throws, I called another time-out. I told our guys that he was going to miss both free throws and that we would get the rebound. Of course, I prayed this would happen, but I had no clue. I told our players to get the rebound and to run a set play that would give us the winning shot. I looked them all in the eyes and said, "Guys, we are going to win this game." I guess they believed me because the ham-fisted colossus missed both free throws, and we got the rebound.

There were six ticks on the clock. The fans were hysterical. Our point guard began casually dribbling the ball up the court. Five. Four. Three. He crossed half court. Two. I screamed at him to shoot the ball. If he did not shoot the ball before the buzzer, he would walk the 300 miles back to our campus. Scratch that. He wouldn't be able to walk. One. Please, Dear God, don't make me kill him! He took the shot. From thirty feet. Why did he not get closer? He had time. Zero. The buzzer sounded while the ball was in the air. Prayers and promises wafted from the stands toward heaven. Prayers and even more promises hurried to the abode of God from our bench. Creepy silence. Thousands of eyes watched the ball slowly rotate through the air. Bated breath. Pressure. Everything felt like slow motion.

Have you ever wondered what guardian angels do in their spare time? What do they do to pass the time when they are not protecting you from traffic accidents and dog bites? My angel plays basketball. I know because he put the ball through the net.

I went delirious. We won! They followed the plan, and we really, truly won. I can't recall what happened for the next few minutes. I vaguely remember a weird dance. It was not pretty. There is video evidence, but I still maintain plausible deniability.

When writing your budget, you should plan how you intend to spend your money. You must plan to tithe. You will never give bring to God what he owns if you wait until after all the bills get paid. God demands to be first anyway. When I prioritize and plan, then I will do the things I prearranged to do. It won't happen unless I make it happen.

Saving for retirement and the future, learning contentment, and living with financial blessing should begin with a clear view of who God is and who you are in Christ. God gives peace. Worry, stress, and discontentment come from jealousy and pride. Contentment will keep us from unplanned spending, but it does not happen by chance. You must plan to be contented. We execute that plan by focusing on God, His blessings, and how thankful we are for what we have.

Write Out Your Financial Goals

The wise look ahead to see what is coming, but fools deceive themselves. Proverbs 14:8[51]

If you do not write down your objectives, you will probably never achieve them. We tend to stray from goals we don't read or see on a regular basis. Write down your financial strategy, and then go over it with your family at the beginning of each month. This action holds everyone accountable and creates buy-in. Make sure to write specific goals.

- **I want to tithe starting ...**
- **I want to be debt-free by ...**
- **I want to buy a house by...**
- **I want to start a business by...**
- **I want to retire by ...**
- **I want to vacation at...**

51 Proverbs 14:8, NLT

I am not a financial expert. I do not have a television or radio show about money, and I certainly do not have a degree in economics. But I can totally understand the practical truth Solomon gave us; stop daydreaming and start doing. That is not complicated. It does not take an advanced degree to comprehend it. You don't even have to be very smart to get it. There is no doubt that it is brilliant, though.

The Bible presents profound yet simple choices that we must make. Stop dreaming and start doing. There is no doubt that something unplanned will happen to you. It is not a matter of *if* but a matter of *when*. Wise people prepare for the inevitable, the unexpected, and the unplanned. Foolish people do not get ready. They sit around and hope for the best and live on wishful thinking and daydreams. Some people like to live in a pretend world. Cars break down, kids grow up, and stuff wears out. Some people think God is mad at them when normal stuff happens. He is not. He just tells us to plan for life.

We must face the facts of life and plan for the unknowable, the inevitable, and the unexpected. Save for the future. Spend less that what you make because you are going to need margin in your finances for the unforeseen. Plan on it, and then you will be ready when it happens. Stop dreaming and make your plan now.

Talk with Your Wife

1. *Do you have savings for unexpected events, like car repairs, appliance repairs, or a trip to the emergency room?*
2. *Discuss how much money you should save for unexpected events. (Many experts recommend $2500)*
3. *What debts do you need to pay off before you can save and create financial margin?*
4. *Write out your financial goals together.*
5. *Pray for God to help you commit to a financial plan.*

DAY EIGHTEEN

Generous People are Happy People

What happens when we allow pride and materialism to creep into our lives? We get filled with covetousness and envy. We become discontented with our personal lives. We start to feel unhappy and empty. We can't really identify what we want, but we always feel that it is just out of our reach. Unchecked, these feelings often lead to a debt trap. We think that we must spend our way into happiness. Failing to agree with God about our materialistic mindset hinders our spiritual growth. Jesus talked about discovering "true wealth" through a right relationship with God and money. He tied spirituality to money management. It truly is a spiritual exercise to see your money God's way.

The Cost of Happiness

Several years ago, when our three children were in elementary school, I was out of town for a speaking engagement. I called home to speak with Kim, and she informed me that the fair recently arrived in town. The kids were begging to go. It really got my attention when she said, "It is free to get into the fair." I figured I could not lose with this scenario. It was free entertainment. It would make the kids happy. It would make Kim happy because they would stop pestering her for a couple of hours. It most certainly made me happy because it was free. I saw a win-win-win scenario.

What Kim told me about "getting in for free" was technically accurate. It did not cost anything to enter the fair. But it did cost something to enjoy it. The admission was free. But if you wanted cotton candy, candy apples, drinks, or to ride the roller coaster and the contraptions that spin until you get sick, then it cost you something.

This principle applies to the Christian life. Getting into the family of God is free. At least, it is free to us. It cost God a lot, but we get the gift of eternal life by faith. However, enjoying the Christian life is not free. Make no mistake; the blessings of enjoying the Christian life far outweigh the costs. There is no greater life than a life lived for Jesus. Just make sure that you understand that a blessed life is not free of charge. You must invest obedience to get all the enjoyment out of it.

The Bible teaches that generous people are happy people. Jesus told us that we are more blessed when we give than when we receive.[52] There are many ways this is true for us. We are happier when we obey. We are happier when we live under God's financial provision and blessing. We are happier when we are selfless. We are happier when we have financial margin. We are happier when we invest in God's kingdom. We are happier when we make a difference. We are happier when we release material things and seek spiritual things.

I learned this principle at a young age. My parents taught me to tithe when I was only ten years old. I tithed my weekly allowance. As I got older and began to work and learn the value of money, it was easy to continue tithing. I discovered the power of generosity. By my senior year of

52 Acts 20:35

high school, I had purchased a car and had saved enough money to pay for my first year of college. Just a few weeks before I was supposed to leave for college, a missionary came to our church. I felt that God clearly led me to give everything in my bank account to support the work this missionary did. You can imagine how that tested my faith. One week later I got a phone call from a total stranger, and he paid my entire tuition, room, and board for four years of college.

Jesus said that money management and spiritual growth are connected. I can't tell you how much I grew spiritually through that experience. The old proverb holds life-altering truth; "You can't out-give God." I learned that generous people are the happiest and most blessed people in the world.

Talk with Your Wife

1. *Can you identify any spirit of materialism in your marriage?*
2. *What are your greatest financial fears?*
3. *In what ways do you consider yourself generous?*
4. *The Bible teaches that the tithe – the first ten percent – belongs to God. Tithing is giving to God what is already his. We don't start giving until we give offerings above the tithe. Using the biblical standard, how generous are you?*
5. *Pray together and ask God to give you a true spirit of generosity. Ask Him to reveal to you how much He loves you and ask Him to help you become generous and happy.*

PART FIVE

Grace-Centered Parenting

My parents were fans of corporeal punishment. I remember getting spanked with a switch on more than one occasion. If you think a switch is what is used to turn a light on and off, then you are not from the South. A switch is a long, thin tree branch. It is about half the width of your pinkie finger and is usually about three feet long. It makes a distinct swooshing sound as it whips through the air. The sound is just as scary as the actual spanking. Switches don't do any damage, but they sting and are a useful disciplinary tool, especially for young boys filled with mischief.

When I was twelve years old, I did not get many spankings, which was a remarkable improvement from my earlier years. I had matured enough that I did not need that kind of correction, for the most part. I guess this day was an exception. I don't remember what I did to make my mom so upset, but evidently, I crossed the proverbial line. With reprobation in her eyes, she told me, "Go get a switch. I'm going to spank you." When a man can choose the implement of his correction, he has a sacred duty to choose the least offensive, painful, and corrective instrument possible. I thought I chose wisely. I came back with a green twig, barely six inches long. Evidently, that was not the wisest choice in my mom's eyes. Her wrath reached biblical proportions as she told me to get something more appropriate. She said I would regret it if I did not come back with something bigger.

So, I did. I found my dad's ax and chopped down a young tree. It was about fourteen feet tall. I hewed the branches and walked into our kitchen dragging the felled timber behind me. It did not even fit in the room, but I stood there smiling at my mom and asked, "Is this big enough?" She tried to hide it but she could not. She began to laugh hysterically. In her kindness, she did not give me what I deserved. I have been a big fan of grace ever since.

DAY NINETEEN

Good Parenting Begins with Grace

I can remember the powerful feelings I had when our children were born. God favored Kim and me with three beautiful gifts; Brittney, Brandon, and Brooke. The emotions I experienced with each birth were profound. I knew that I was going to love them for the rest of my life. They were the most beautiful babies I had ever seen. I felt a profound sense of responsibility to be the best father I could be. I knew that I had to do my best to love and protect them. I also knew that I needed a lot of help.

Good parenting begins with God's grace. When one starts with God's undeserved favor, then you realize that perfect parenting is impossible, but also that you are just the parent God had in mind when He gave you the delightful gift of children. God chose to give your kids to you to demonstrate his love and so you could show His grace to them in return.

King David wrote a passage of scripture that illustrates this beautifully. We know from reading the Bible that David wasn't a perfect man or a perfect parent. But you can feel God's grace in the psalm he wrote about his son, Solomon. Solomon represents God's grace to David after he had failed morally with Bathsheba. I love how he penned these words:

> Unless the Lord builds a house, the work of the builders is wasted. Unless the Lord protects a city, guarding it with sentries will do no good. It is useless for you to work so hard from early morning

> until late at night, anxiously working for food to eat; for God gives rest to his loved ones. Children are a gift from the Lord; they are a reward from him. Children born to a young man are like arrows in a warrior's hands. How joyful is the man whose quiver is full of them! He will not be put to shame when he confronts his accusers at the city gates.[53]

Building a family is like building a house. If we try to mold a godly household apart from the truth of God's Word, we waste our time. You can't build a Christian life apart from God's grace, and neither can you build a Christian home apart from it. When we rest in God's grace to train our children, then we recognize that God is the one who does the work. That doesn't mean that you have no role or responsibility in parenting. It just means that resting in God's grace is a critical component in parenting. Stop worrying and start resting in Him. All the worry in the world will not protect your children. But God can and will when we rest in Him.

Parents are like warriors and children are like arrows. The primary job of the champion archer is to make sure that the arrow hits the target; otherwise, the arrows are useless. Do you get the picture? Your primary job as a parent is to get your children to the right target. What is the target? A degree in medicine? A large house in the suburbs? A sports career? Manners? While those things may be desirable, the destination pictured here is a relationship

53 Psalm 127:1-5

with God, or to be more specific, a relationship with Jesus Christ. Education, wealth, health and manners are important, but they are not the most important. The most important thing you can do for your child is to point him or her to the correct target.

Thinking of parenting in this way makes your job much simpler. If you are going to be an effective warrior, then you need to pay attention to some important principles.

Arrows Must Be Released

You can't completely control an arrow, but you can guide it. You must let go at the right time, or it will not hit the target. For many parents, releasing their children is a difficult thing. We want to protect our children from pain, harm, and mishap. To be sure, this is a part of a parent's job, but we must be willing to let them experience failure, pain, and disappointment for them to get prepared for life. Faith empowers you to release properly. You must prepare them like a spiritual warrior and then deliver them to God. Of course, we are talking about releasing them to God, not abdicating our responsibility to lead and train them.

Arrows Must Be Aimed

Failing to point precisely causes the arrow to miss the target. Aiming at the wrong thing does more harm than good. In a battle, warriors don't aim at random targets, but at well-chosen ones. A soldier can successfully nail the bullseye in the sweet spot, but if he has selected the wrong target, his work is all in vain. In the same way, we can act "target challenged" when we get our children involved in every activity under the sun except those that teach them to honor God. The real goal is a relationship with Jesus Christ.

Arrows Must Be Timed

Part of a proper release involves good timing. Otherwise, the arrow will never hit its target. Even if your bow is aligned properly, the arrow will not reach the goal if you release it at the wrong time. Let go too early, and it will lodge in the ground; release it too late, and it will sail over the target. We must release our children to God, but we must also let go at the right time.

Good parenting requires continuously releasing our children to God. We must release them early into his care. All our efforts and worries are in vain unless we release them into a relationship with Christ. We must also release them all along the way as they grow up. We must release them into learning responsibility, helping them become accountable for their actions, and learning how to handle failure and success. We must release them into spiritual maturity. Our faith should point them to Christ, but it can't take the place of a personal, growing relationship with him. When it becomes appropriate, we must release them into adulthood. You are still the warrior, but your role will change at that point. As your children grow up, serve God, and get married, you are no longer responsible for releasing arrows. You then release warriors.

Allow the Lord to build your home with His grace.

Talk with Your Wife

1. *Talk with your wife about the role of the church in your family life.*
2. *How can you pray effectively for your children?*
3. *Talk about how you can release your children toward a relationship with Christ.*
4. *Pray for your family. Ask God to make you a powerful warrior/parent and to help your kids reach the right target in life.*

DAY TWENTY

Dealing with Pain as a Parent

A loving father allows his son to feel pain. That may seem like an absurd statement since we know that one of the ways love gets expressed is by protecting the object of our love. How can love inflict pain on purpose? It can when the experience helps our children avoid greater hurt, sorrow, and damage. We observe this act of love in nature. A mother eagle will push the eaglet from the comfort and safety of its nest even when it may be dangerous to do so. This shocking act is necessary for the eaglet to learn to fly. Temporary fear and pain are far less cruel than confining an eagle to a nest because eagles are made to fly. So are you.

Striking a balance between protection and preparation is one of the primary tasks of a parent. You must manage the friction through prayer and wisdom. Too much and you risk alienation and bitterness. Too little and you hamstring your child with a puny soul that is unprepared for life and unable to navigate conflict and disappointment.

Our Heavenly Father is greater than any earthly parent could ever be. He is far wiser and loving than human mothers and fathers. God wants to prepare you to live courageously and to release your soul into wide-open spaces, unfettered by fear, and thirsty for life. He loves us enough to give us sufficient pain to keep us vigilant while draping His arm around our shoulder the whole time. Grief and disappointment often open the door for the greatest ministry to others and the closest fellowship with Christ.

Pain is inevitable. Anyone who tries to paint a picture of a future in this present darkness that is devoid of pain or disappointment is being dishonest. Such existence lives only in fairy tales, not in real life. On the other hand, God does not want us to live in worry or fear. He has our back. He knows what is best for us. We must not let moments of disappointment define our lives. I am convinced that good is greater than evil, joy is stronger than sadness, happiness overcomes despair, and love conquers hate. God marked life with overwhelming love when Jesus came and died a propitious death for our sins. He wins. When we dance to the rhythm of His grace, no fear, sorrow, or pain can control us.

Parenting pain trickles into every parent's soul from time to time. I am not suggesting that the pain you feel from your children outweighs the joy of having children. No parent believes that. But you will feel pain. It is how you deal with it that makes the difference. There will be pain from your schedule, your sacrifice, and your lack of sleep. Hurt comes from disappointment and disobedience. There will even be anxiety in your relationship with your children on occasion.

Job experienced the ultimate pain of losing seven sons and three daughters in a single day. In the middle of his trial, he asked a question that each of us should ask ourselves. Will I take the good from God but not the bad?[54] Will I accuse God of failing me when bad things happen?

54 Job 2:10

The Apostle Paul gave us the answer when he wrote, "Give thanks in all circumstances; for this is the will of God in Christ Jesus for you."[55]

Therein lies the answer to dealing with the pain and disappointment that we inevitably face. Learn to be thankful in every situation. When things get tough, remember the good. When you are tired, count your blessings. God's will for us always results in our ultimate blessing and brings glory to Him. Why? One reason is that it makes our situation better.

I hope you are not experiencing tough times right now. If you are, I hope they are short-lived. I hope you can learn what God is teaching you about His character and that you see, through the eyes of faith, what He is preparing you to do for His glory. If you find yourself facing immediate or imminent pain, then thank Him for the pain and disappointment. That is the first step to recovering your joy and turning what the enemy means for harm into something that God can use for His glory.

55 1 Thessalonians 5:18

Talk with Your Wife

1. *Tell your wife how you are thankful for her and ask her to tell you how she is thankful for you.*
2. *Think of as many things as you can to thank God for about your children. Say them out loud. Include the good and the bad and give God your worries about your family. Ask Him to increase your faith.*
3. *Say a prayer of thanks together.*

DAY TWENTY-ONE

Making Wise Scheduling Choices

King Solomon was declared to be the wisest man in the ancient world. His wisdom came from God. According to him, smart choices and common sense are necessary ingredients for a healthy household. He wrote, "Homes are built on the foundation of wisdom and understanding."[56] Not every choice that we make for our family is a simple matter of right and wrong. Many of the most important decisions come down to making wise choices. Some choices are not sinful, but they are not wise. We often struggle with making unwise decisions, especially when it comes to schedules and activities.

The Okefenokee Swamp is a major wetlands park and attraction that has hundreds of miles of pristine canoe and boat trails. It is a nature lover's paradise. The park is also home to many alligators. During the early 90's I took a group of teenagers on a canoeing excursion to this lovely part of God's creation. I warned everyone about the dangers of alligators and told the students to stay in their canoes. I told them not to feed the alligators, not to throw things at the alligators (alligators have feelings too), not to try and swim with the alligators, and not to throw their friends into the water where the alligators were lurking. Being a pastor, I used this opportunity to talk to them about making wise choices.

Not surprisingly, two of the high school boys ignored my message. They chose, instead, to stand in their canoe and channel their inner gladiator. It was the battle of the

56 Proverbs 24:3, GNB

paddles. Before I could point out that there was a gator lying on the bank about twenty feet away, their canoe capsized, and they both fell into the water. The giant reptile immediately hit the water and headed straight for the boys and their overturned boat. You can imagine my horror. What would I tell their parents?

I know that Jesus could walk on water, and Peter gave it a shot for a few seconds, but I am convinced that no one else has defied the laws of physics and gravity until that day. How else could I explain how they got into my boat so quickly? Maybe everyone can be like Jesus when properly motivated.

Parents often make unwise choices that eventually come back to bite them. How many times do poor scheduling choices bring negative long-term consequences? Often the choice is not between right and wrong but between the wise and the unwise. Making sound decisions with your family schedule is essential for you and your children. To which activities do you say yes? To which do you say no? How much time should you allow your kids to spend in extracurricular activities? Is spending five or six nights a week chauffeuring your child to practices and games quality family time? What does missing church because of a baseball game say to your child? Is it possible that otherwise wholesome things are robbing your family? What priorities are you teaching your sons and daughters?

Be Wise in Your Schedule

Scripture tells us that we have a responsibility to ourselves and to God to make wise choices regarding our time. We must carefully consider what we prioritize. I do not believe that sports and extracurricular activities are wrong. I believe that they are beneficial and helpful if you make sure to prioritize the right things in life. The most important must come first every day, or it will get marginalized without your being aware of it. Paul the Apostle understood this when he wrote, "Look carefully then how you walk, not as unwise but as wise, making the best use of the time, because the days are evil. Therefore do not be foolish, but understand what the will of the Lord is."[57]

Allowing our scheduling choices to sideline, devalue, and disregard the important things in life is easier than you might think. We typically do not intend for that to happen. For most families, the activities that crowd out their perceived priorities are usually not bad or evil. To win this spiritual tug-of-war, you must fight for what is right. You must choose between what is good and what is best. You should put the big things in first: church attendance, giving, serving, time with God, and family time. Otherwise, you will sacrifice the truly important on the altar of the immediate.

57 Ephesians 5:15–17.

Create Margin

Trying to fit more and more into your schedule is tempting. When we regularly add without ever subtracting anything, we deceive ourselves into thinking that we have the time and energy to get it all done. That is not realistic. There certainly will be times when we will be busier than others. However, if we never create a margin in our lives, we will eventually burn out or stop doing something important. Operating with a margin means that you don't over schedule yourself or your children. Success requires learning to say no. Say yes to the important things and say no to things that rob you of blessing and margin.

Ultimately, the decision to simplify your schedule comes down to faith. The Bible teaches us to trust God with our schedule. By committing our time to God and putting him first in our schedules, we rest in God's grace. That was the purpose of the Sabbath. By committing to rest and worship one day a week, you are saying to God that you trust Him. I can get more done in six "blessed days" than I can in seven days that are not blessed. Once you begin to trust God with your schedule, you will discover grace and margin. You will have less stress and more energy for the things that are most important.

Talk with Your Wife

1. *What are the things that you consider to be most important for your family life?*
2. *Does your schedule reflect those priorities?*
3. *What could you do to create more of a margin in your life?*
4. *Pray for each other and ask God to increase your faith to help you trust Him with your schedule. Ask God for the faith to make the right choices for your family.*

PART SIX

The Naked Truth About Your Sex Life

Kim and I had been married for about a year when we bought our first house. One day I got home early and pulled my car into the garage and shut the door behind me. Since we did not have an automatic garage door opener, we usually left the garage door open until the other person came home.

Not on this day.

I hid in the closet in our bedroom waiting for her to arrive. I heard her come in and piddle around the kitchen for a few minutes. My heart was pounding with anticipation. Finally, she came into the bedroom and opened her closet. I grabbed her and screamed like a banshee…so did she. In my newlywed thinking, I thought I had scored. I won!

I learned that is not how women keep score. In fact, I failed to score for a long time after that.

That was not the smartest thing I ever did. I lived in the doghouse for a while. On a positive note, it did give Kim a chance to practice having a forgiving spirit. It also gave me an opportunity to "gain wisdom" as it says in Proverbs.

Since we discuss sex in this section, husbands, you probably flipped to this part of the book first. Make sure to read from the beginning. It will help you get the most out of this section. I promise if you work on the things discussed in the first five chapters, then you will have a better sex life.

DAY TWENTY-TWO

A Redeemed Sex Life

Many men want to know how to have more sex, and many women want to know how to make their husband more romantic. Sex and romance are a huge part of the human experience. God created us in His image and designed us to have relationships. In more than three decades of pastoral ministry, I have discovered that sex and money are two of the biggest interests in most people's lives. They are also two of the greatest sources of problems and tensions in our lives.

Everyone is interested in sex, but few understand what the Bible teaches about it. When you obey what the culture teaches us about sex, then you reap the obsessions and problems facing our world. But when you follow God's plan and understand his purpose for sex and human sexuality, then you can have a blessed sex life.

A Redeemed Sex Life

Jesus Christ came into this world to die for our sins and redeem us back to God. It is through His sacrifice that God puts us in right standing with Him. When Jesus paid the price for you, He did so to redeem all your life. Christ died for more than your past; He also died for your future. The Son of God died to redeem every part of your life, including your sex life.

What does it mean to have a redeemed sex life? It means that you live as a blood-bought believer, that your sins and past are forgiven and redeemed by Jesus, and that you now follow God's plan for your life. You live under Divine blessings.

Sex and Romance in a Christian Home

God created us to have relationships because He made us in His image. The husband and wife relationship, romance, and sex were God's ideas. God performed the first marriage in the Garden of Eden. Since we are fallen creatures, however, we can take what God planned as a blessing and get it wrong.

Fortunately, the Bible speaks about sex and romance quite a lot. Genesis and Song of Solomon teach us some marvelous insights about how to connect, communicate, live openly with each other, and build a Christian home. Ephesians, Colossians, and 1 Peter also teach us how to treat each other and live together in a way that produces a happy home. But I want to focus on a passage of scripture that is incredibly helpful for married people. God's love for us is evident in this passage.

> Now concerning the matters about which you wrote: "It is good for a man not to have sexual relations with a woman." But because of the temptation to sexual immorality, each man should have his own wife and each woman her own husband. The husband should give to his wife her conjugal rights, and likewise the wife to her husband. For the wife does not have authority over her own body, but the

> husband does. Likewise the husband does not have authority over his own body, but the wife does. Do not deprive one another, except perhaps by agreement for a limited time, that you may devote yourselves to prayer; but then come together again, so that Satan may not tempt you because of your lack of self-control.[58]

We can glean two powerful and important truths from this passage that show how God redeems our sex lives.

Principle #1 - We Must Conform to God's Word Rather Than Culture

First, believers must follow God's instructions from the Bible rather than the inane and inconsistent philosophies of the culture. The Corinthian believers faced cultural myths and trivial attitudes toward sex during their day. They had many questions about sexual behavior. They asked Paul about a well-circulated idea at the time, which stated that husbands and wives should not have regular sexual relations. He responded, "Now concerning the matters about which you wrote: 'It is good for a man not to have sexual relations with a woman.'" Some people in that culture taught that sex was evil. Paul corrected their thinking by showing what God teaches about the subject. Our culture has many erroneous beliefs about sex too, so we can learn much from what he wrote. Here are a few things we can learn about human sexuality from God's Word.

58 1 Corinthians 7:1-5, ESV

- **God created us in his image – male and female.**

He addressed husbands and wives. These are two very distinct but equal roles. Genesis teaches us that our roles and perspectives are an important part of His plan. The differences in the sexes reflect God's love for us and His blessings. Confusing your role leads to problems.

- **God created sex for a purpose.**

Paul gave God's perspective on sex between a husband and wife. God's first commands to Adam and Eve in Genesis were to eat, work, and have sex – "be fruitful and multiply and fill the earth." These commands show us that our sex lives are to fulfill the gospel. God commanded us to fill the earth with worshippers of him. He gave this incredible blessing for having children, pleasure, romance, love, connection, intimacy, dependency, openness, and communion. Any sex act that does not reflect the gospel can't possibly bring blessings.

- **You can have a God-blessed sex life.**

In the passage, he wrote that husband and wife are, "To give conjugal rights." The Greek word from which this phrase is translated served as a financial term. It means to pay a debt, to fulfill an obligation or duty, and to give respect and honor. He stated that our spouse has authority over our body. He wrote, "Do not deprive one another." It means do not, "cause to suffer loss, rob or steal, prevent from a benefit, defraud, or take away." What does this passage teach us about a God-blessed sex life?

- Sex is to be a mutual expression of love between husband and wife.
- Sex is to be decided upon together.
- Sex must be about serving my spouse's needs.
- Sex must never function as a weapon to manipulate.
- Sex must respect and honor my spouse.
- Sex protects my spouse from temptation.
- Sex is never to be abusive.
- Prayer leads to better sex! Serving God together leads to better sex!

Principle #2 - Sex Must Mirror the Gospel

The second principle is just as powerful as the first. From the beginning of creation, God designed sex to display the beauty of the gospel. Your sex life significantly affects your spiritual life. In the context surrounding 1 Corinthians 7:1-5 Paul wrote that our bodies are the dwelling place of the Holy Spirit. Believers must walk with God passionately and live out His purpose. In other words, we are to live out the gospel in all areas of life.

The only way we can live out the gospel is to build our lives around God's grace. It must be the center of our thinking. It can't be just a Sunday thing, but it must be an everyday thing – even in our marital relationships. It is through God's grace that we fulfill our purpose and find meaning in life. God gives the grace to help us in our time of need. He forgives because of Jesus and restores what the enemy has taken. He blesses our faith in Him and heals our deepest wounds. No matter what your past has been, you can find His grace to help your marriage and in every area of your life.

God designed every part of creation to show His love and unfathomable grace toward us. Marriage was God's idea, and it illustrates the relationship between Christ and the church. You can have a God-blessed marriage. You can have a glorified romantic life when you follow His design, care for each other, serve each other, and keep Christ at the center of your marriage. Knowing what we know about our culture and all the sexual problems we face, don't you think God's ways are best?

Talk with Your Wife

1. *Talk about your sex life. Many people find this awkward, but it should not be between husband and wife. Do not be defensive. Ask your spouse how often he or she thinks you should have sex.*
2. *Sex must not be exclusively about self-fulfillment according to 1 Corinthians chapter seven. Ask how you can better serve your spouse. What does he or she like or dislike? What can you do to acknowledge that your body belongs to your spouse?*
3. *Do you think you have a redeemed sex life? Is it in the image of God?*
4. *Prayer can make sex better! Pray with each other every day and discover if this makes you closer, more intimate, and more open to each other.*

DAY TWENTY-THREE

A Grace-Centered Sex Life

God's grace can do in a moment more than you can do in a lifetime. More than you need counseling, or a seminar, or a book, you need God's grace. Grace is his undeserved, unearned, unmerited kindness and favor. Marriages that are grace-centered are better.

Our culture portrays marriage as a place of self-fulfillment. In the self-obsessed society in which we live, self-fulfillment sits atop the list of things humanity worships. When marriage ceases to be self-fulfilling, as it obviously does apart from a strong commitment to serving one another, people want out. Suddenly, you no longer feel "in love," so you justify ditching the marriage and searching for the next fantasy that fulfills you. I believe marriage can and should be fulfilling. But the key to a fulfilling marriage is not selfishly focusing on your individual needs, but selflessly focusing on the needs of your spouse. Self-denial is a fundamental component of a happy marriage according to the Bible.

Submission Releases God's Grace in My Life and Marriage

How do you get more of God's grace in your marriage? As strange as it may seem, you release grace by submitting. I want to take the word submission – a word that so many hate, fear, and misunderstand - and show you how it holds the key to God's blessings and grace in your marriage. And yes, it also leads to a better sex life because it leads to a better marriage.

The Apostle Peter demonstrated how this works when he wrote, "God opposes the proud but gives grace to the humble."[59] Having humility means that you submit. It is the opposite of pride. It is admitting that you are not the source of strength, goodness, and success but God is. This verse is a quote from Proverbs 3:34 which states, "Toward the scorners he is scornful, but to the humble he gives favor." A scorner is a mocker, a person who is proud and haughty. The literal translation of the word means "to make mouths at." Through mutual submission, husbands and wives do not "make mouths" at each other through sarcasm, hurtful words, rebellion, or selfish demands. God's grace gets released in the greatest measure to marriages in which both spouses submit to each other.

Submission Begins with Christ

In Ephesians chapter five, the Apostle Paul admonished Christian spouses to submit to each other as they would to Christ. Part of the chapter famously tells wives to submit to their husbands. Perhaps men have focused on that part so much that they forgot to read the rest of the text. It tells husbands to love their wives in the same way that Christ loved the church. He submitted to the will of the Father and gave Himself freely for us. That is the greatest example of submission in the Bible. It is impossible for that passage to mean that only women are to submit to their husbands. Men are to yield to the needs of their wives as well. Especially since in the same part of the letter it states,

59 1 Peter 5:5, ESV

"Submit to one another out of reverence for Christ."[60] Only when we submit to Christ are we able to have the self-denial to yield to our spouse. We must follow Christ's example.

Submission does not create subservience, dominance, or designate value. It is a willfully designed decision, on your own part, to sacrifice and to put someone else's good and his or her needs ahead of your own. This is not coerced, or bought, but freely given. It is holy. It is required for the kind of loving marriage that the Bible commands us to have. This kind of marriage requires imitating Christ's love and submission. By putting your spouse's needs ahead of your own you release the flow of God's grace in your marriage.

Think of how Jesus demonstrated this for us. When He was twelve years old, He spoke to the rabbis, and they were amazed at His knowledge. The young Messiah submitted to them by asking questions respectfully and in humility. He knew that He was the Word of God. Jesus knew the Old Testament scriptures because they were from Him and about him. How incredible is it that he submitted to the rabbis and deferred to his parents even though he was God the Son? The next part of the story tells us that God released to Jesus wisdom, stature, and favor with God and man. The obvious lesson is that submission releases favor and grace.

60 Ephesians 5:21, NIV

What Does Grace Do for Your Marriage?

When God releases grace into your marriage, then He begins to build it for you. He will restore and heal broken relationships. He will work *on* your family and *for* it. God will make right all the things that have been wrong in your marriage. He will strengthen you and rekindle your love. God will build your resolve and patience through his grace. His grace will do the same things in your marriage that He does for you in salvation.

Marriages held together by human effort can only last so long. But through grace, God promises to help you. He will build, restore, and work for your growth. But we must submit to Christ and each other. When you do that, God releases power and blessings into your marriage. Submission is the starting place for God's blessings!

Talk with Your Wife

1. *Ask your wife how you can meet her emotional needs.*
2. *Talk to each other about submitting to Christ.*
3. *Ask each other how you can serve the other well.*
4. *Pray that God helps you both understand how to submit to one another.*

DAY TWENTY-FOUR

Better Sex Protects Your Marriage

In my years of ministry, I have observed that the percentage of Christians who have affairs is not significantly different than the percentage of non-Christians who have affairs. That is astounding to me. What does it mean? While that observation is by no means scientific, it does make me ask why so many Christians have affairs? On the one hand, you could make the argument that many Christians justify their sins and ignore the teaching of the Bible. But isn't that true of non-Christians as well?

We are all made in God's image. Even though we have a sin nature, believers and nonbelievers share certain characteristics, like the desire for love, community, beauty, and justice. These God-infused traits abide in believers and non-believers alike. Having an affair is not normal and violates our innate nature as human beings. We don't have to be taught that it is wrong to cheat. We know it intuitively. Can it be that breaking one's marriage vows stems from more than boredom or rebellion? Could it be that it is a misplaced search for meaning and love? Could it be because we worship ourselves rather than God? I would argue that breaking the eighth Commandment is difficult to do while worshipping God in spirit and truth.

No matter what you think about my observations, you probably concur that having an affair is wrong. How can you avoid this devastating mistake?

Know It Can Happen to You

Glossing over something is not a way to deal with it. We must be aware of our vulnerabilities if we want to avoid having an affair. The Apostle Paul warned us to consider that we are vulnerable to temptation, no matter how mature we think we are. One of the first steps for avoiding an affair is to recognize your vulnerability. Learn to build healthy boundaries. That is why I never counsel alone, have a meal alone, or ride in a car alone with a woman who is not a family member. I remember when one of my female staff members had car trouble about a mile from our church. I recognized her while driving to the church office. I stopped, made sure she was OK, and then drove to the church and found two people to go and help her. That may be a bit extreme, but it is a policy that has protected me for many years.

Be Aware of the Effects of an Affair

Affairs are devastating. I can't adequately describe the pain I have witnessed from affairs. They devastate families, children, and finances. Affairs cripple people emotionally and create future trust issues. It is impossible to translate the sensational feelings one has during an affair into a long-term relationship. The salacious scandal creates euphoria. The secret nature of it can't be sustained in a real-life marriage. Covert excitement gets replaced by the normalcy of everyday life. The new slowly fades. You find the same struggles and problems in your new relationship that you had in your previous marriage. The difference is that now, you have the added stress of divorce, alimony, child support, conflict, and a divided income. Breaking your marriage vows violates a sacred trust. Hebrews 13:4 states, "Honor marriage, and guard the *sacredness* of sexual intimacy between wife and husband."[61]

God's Commands Protect Us

Every command in the Bible is rooted in God's love for us. They do not create pain but protect us, and bring pleasure and joy to our lives. Sex is an Image of God thing. 1 Timothy 4:4 states, "For everything God created is good, and nothing is to be rejected, but all is to be received with a prayer of thanks."[62] The word "everything" includes sex in marriage.

Having an affair is a spiritual issue. Everything in the Christian life is directly related to how we worship God. I believe that the Bible is highly practical. Too many people see the Bible as mysterious and think only a few can understand it. That simply is not true. The Bible does not just give prohibitions but practical steps to live your life in a positive way.

61 Hebrews 13:4, MES

62 1 Timothy 4:4, GNT

Seek to Understand

In 1 Peter 3:7 the Apostle Peter wrote an amazing and practical truth for husbands and wives. He stated that it is possible for husbands and wives to understand each other better. In fact, the command was that we must learn to understand each other better. Knowing that it is possible to understand each other is good news for every married person.

This truth is very practical for married couples. Peter was saying that it is possible to learn about the emotional, physical, and spiritual needs of your spouse. While the differences between men and women are a part of the joy of marriage – the mystery of marriage if you will – the differences are not so great that we can't learn how to understand each other.

Bolster Your Commitment

Anything that suffers neglect gets worse. This truth applies to your health, your finances, your business, or even trivial things such as your golf game. Your marriage is no exception, and you must work on your relationship. It, like everything else in life, is vulnerable to inattention and carelessness. I believe the most significant commitment in marriage is your commitment to God. You are meant to worship in a church together, to give together, and to serve together. Being involved together in regular worship, service, and small group community is critical. Do people who do these things ever have affairs? Yes, but I believe it is because they neglect an important underlying principle – worshipping God. Committing to God's values requires following and obeying Him. Psalm 119:9, NLT Psalm 119:9 states, "How can a young person stay pure? By obeying your word."[63]

Guard Against Temptation

You must establish the kind of boundaries that will keep you from giving in to temptation. Experiencing temptation is not a sin, but exposing ourselves to constant and needless provocation is unwise. One of the best ways to avoid having an affair is to work on your sex life in your marriage. As was written earlier, the Apostle Paul instructed husbands and wives to engage in marital sex regularly. Your body belongs to your spouse. He indicated that healthy sexual intimacy in marriage helps overcome the temptation to cheat. It draws couples closer together emotionally, physically and spiritually. Godly sex between a husband and wife is an act of worship.

63 Psalm 119:9, NLT

Talk with Your Wife

1. *Talk about what tempts you with your wife. Ask about her temptations.*
2. *Talk about boundaries in your marriage. What are the appropriate boundaries?*
3. *Ask your spouse how you can help with temptations and boundaries.*
4. *Pray for each other. Ask God to bless your sex life.*

DAY TWENTY-FIVE

God Wants You to Have Great Sex

We have learned some biblical values about marriage and sex. Now let's bring it all together. In my experience, most people in our culture have a skewed view of sex. Those who are not committed Christians (and many who are) believe that God's only command about sex is, "Don't do it!" Most believe that if you follow the teachings found in the Bible, you will miss out and never have any fun. That kind of thinking is rooted in biblical ignorance or a misunderstanding of what the Bible truly says.

First, let me clarify what I mean by the term "great sex" in the title of this chapter. When we live according to God's plan and purpose, our lives are better, especially our familial relationships. Research backs up this proposition. Numerous studies have revealed that the most sexually fulfilled and satisfied people are committed to marriage, monogamy, and a relationship with God. Our sex-obsessed culture believes the opposite. They deny the facts because they believe the lies of the enemy! As a result, they miss many blessings that God made available for them.

The writer of Hebrews wrote about how sin brings a false and temporary pleasure. Of course, sinful behavior is fun and easy. Otherwise, we would not be tempted to sin. No one is going to suggest that having an affair, looking at pornography, hooking up with your boyfriend or girlfriend, or going to a strip club is dull and boring. Those things are titillating and exciting...but only for a little while. Eventually, this kind of behavior destroys. It can destroy us physically, emotionally, relationally, and financially. Most of all, it destroys the beauty and intimacy of sex that God designed for us.

Sex Was God's Idea

God has a lot to say about sex. He created it and wanted you to get a blessing from it. All of God's commands bring joy when we follow them, and they express His love for us. Since He is the author of sex and relationships, doesn't it make sense that we should listen to Him rather than the fallen culture?

Previously in this book, we have looked at God's original plan for marriage in Genesis chapters one and two. Let's look at a couple of those passages again.

> "So God created man in his own image, in the image of God he created him; male and female he created them. And God blessed them. And God said to them, 'Be fruitful and multiply and fill the earth...'"[64]

> "Therefore a man shall leave his father and his mother and hold fast to his wife, and they shall become one flesh. And the man and his wife were both naked and were not ashamed."[65]

64 Genesis 1:27-28, ESV

65 Genesis 2:24-25

Notice several principles and purposes we find here:

- His first command was for Adam and Eve to have sex often.
- God blessed sex.
- Blessed sex draws us closer to God in worship.
- Blessed sex reminds us of God's image and purpose.
- Blessed sex is for having children.
- Blessed sex creates strong bonds and unity in your marriage.
- Blessed sex is for pleasure.

God wants to bless your sex life. We are to enjoy as much sex as possible in the bonds of marriage because he planned sex for uniting husbands and wives. Any sex out of wedlock is not blessed, and it has the power to destroy us.

God sees sex as a sacred act. We must not treat it carelessly or casually. According to the writer of Hebrews we are to, "Honor marriage, and guard the sacredness of sexual intimacy between wife and husband. God draws a firm line against casual and illicit sex."[66]

King Solomon wrote, "Let your fountain be blessed, and rejoice in the wife of your youth…Let her breasts fill you at all times with delight; be intoxicated always in her love."[67]

66 Hebrews 13:4, MES

67 Proverbs 5:18-19, ESV

God described sex as intoxicating. Can you imagine that? Who knew that He had so much pleasure and intensity in mind when He designed us to be sexual beings? God planned sex to be fun! That is different than what most people think the Bible teaches about sex. If God intended sex for marriage, then what are married couples to learn about sex? The Bible addresses that in numerous places. I love the little book of Song of Solomon. It is an entire book in the Old Testament about married love, sex, and romance. You should read it!

Sex in marriage is not about manipulation or self-fulfillment but about serving and loving your spouse. God teaches us to view marriage through the lens of the gospel. We are to love sacrificially. Jesus loves us that way. When a man stops manipulating his wife and engages her spiritually, then things work out well for him. When a woman stops using sex as a tool to manipulate her husband and serves him like Christ serves the church, she is more fulfilled and satisfied with her marriage.

God loves you and wants to bless every part of your life; including your sex life! Don't buy the lies of the enemy. Committed Christians have better sex lives because they enjoy the beauty, intimacy, and joy of blessed sex!

Talk with Your Wife

1. *Talk about how the culture has skewed God's view of sex.*
2. *Talk with each other about what you have learned about God's plan for sex.*
3. *How can you enjoy blessed sex?*
4. *Hold you wife and pray for her.*

PART SEVEN

Loving Your Wife for a Lifetime

My Grandpa Phillips scratched his living as a tobacco farmer from the rich but reluctant foothills of North Carolina. His father and grandfather did the same backbreaking labor. Pa Wendell, as I called him, possessed the gift of a silver tongue. He was endlessly entertaining, a captivating storyteller, and possessed a lust for life that made everyone around him feel alive. I loved being around him.

When he was around fifty years of age, he suffered a massive heart attack. It would be the first of several, but he grabbed life by the throat and would not let go until he was 72. During his first heart attack, he lay on the hospital gurney in the emergency room and died. The doctors shocked him back to life twice, and he finally stabilized. My grandmother was hysterical, as you can imagine. When she could see him, she held his hand and with tears in her eyes asked if he saw a light while on death's doorstep. He got a grin on his face and said, "Well, at first, I thought I saw the devil…but I woke up and it was only you."

She slapped him right there in the Intensive Care Unit.

That was their secret to being married for over 50 years. I don't mean the slapping, which was playful by the way, but the fact that they still made each other laugh. They were friends. They laughed and cajoled. Through good times and bad times, they stayed committed. They fell in love as teenagers. When he died over 50 years later, they still loved each other.

DAY TWENTY-SIX

Naked and Proud of It

And the man and his wife were both naked and were not ashamed.[68]

A fascinating thing about the first marriage in the Garden of Eden is how completely open and honest they were with each other. Of course, this was before they ate the forbidden fruit. But think how remarkable that statement is: "The man and his wife were both naked and were not ashamed." That statement contains some beautiful truths and opens a few principles to help us foster a lifelong love.

... the man and his wife

There was a sense of equality between husband and wife. They both were acutely aware of their value to God and each other. They formed a strong team. A team commits to each other, watches out for each other, and sacrifices for the greater good. God designed marriage to be a place of self-sacrifice rather than a place of self-service. Teamwork makes the team work. Teammates do not envy the role of others. They recognize their contribution as valuable and make the team stronger by accepting divinely prescribed roles.

...were both naked

Marriage in the nude gave birth to humanity. Nakedness reveals more than a physical reality. They were completely open with each other. Openness leads to oneness. Absolute acceptance marked their union. Unconditional

68 Genesis 2:25, ESV.

love underpinned their relationship. Until you build a sense of consummate openness and vulnerability with your spouse, you will not experience that kind of God-ordained unity. They did not cover up with each other. There was no shame or embarrassment, but a genuine sense of freedom with each other. Can you imagine that? No jealousy. No striving to get the upper hand. No manipulation. No hurting each other. Openness about struggles and successes, trials and triumphs.

Although it is possible to be uninhibited with each other, the only way you will truly be open is when you rest in the grace of Jesus. Once you understand His grace, then you will give grace more freely. Let's face it, when you are keenly aware that you have done nothing to earn, deserve, or merit His grace, then you can release forgiveness, live with understanding, and love with no strings attached. It mirrors God's love for us. What would happen if we truly began to live by God's grace in our marriage? There would be much less worry and stress. We would be able to communicate more clearly and share our burdens more fully. It would totally revolutionize your marriage.

…and were not ashamed

Shame has vast power. Some suggest that it significantly influences how we act, whom we accept, and how we see ourselves. That is why it is so important to remember that when Christ saves a person, he completely removes the shame of our sins and our past. We must rest in the perfect work of Jesus if we want a Christ-centered marriage. His grace transforms.

Because you are an image-bearer, you can live by grace. You can give and receive grace in your marriage. You can rest in the knowledge that God knew what He was doing when He made you. He makes no mistakes. Resting in Him helps you accept each other. Oddly enough, we often create an illusion of the idealistic partner, rather than embracing the real person. You can't have a perfect spouse, but you can love the one God is sanctifying He continues with his makeover. Women often marry thinking their husband will change. Men often marry thinking their wife will never change. The more we rest in Jesus and his grace, then the more we depend on his finished work to empower our marriage! Resting in him helps you not be ashamed.

Once again, that is not to say that we can expect our spouse to be sinless. No person is without flaws and blemishes, but we can grow and become more like Christ. Although there is no such thing as a perfect marriage, you can have one that is perfect for you!

Don't fall prey to the "soul mate" myth that pervades our culture. Many fear that the person they marry may not be their soul mate, whatever that means. That belief leads to thinking that marriage is a transaction designed for self-fulfillment rather than a biblical relationship requiring love, commitment, sacrifice, and service. A flawed theory like that leads to disappointment because your spouse becomes your idol. You expect your husband or wife to be the answer to all your problems. He or she will fix all that is wrong with your life. You see him or her as the source of your contentment, fulfillment, meaning, security, and hope. Only God can give you those things.

Talk with Your Wife

1. *Ask your wife what she thinks it means to be open with each other.*
2. *Talk with each other about teamwork. How can you both be better teammates?*
3. *What is one thing that brings you shame that you can give to Jesus?*
4. *Although she is not perfect, tell your wife three things you love about her. Let her tell you three things she loves about you.*
5. *Pray together and ask God to let His grace fill your marriage.*

DAY TWENTY-SEVEN

Becoming Friends with Your Spouse

I have performed many wedding ceremonies in my ministry. I often hear a bride and groom describe the other as his or her best friend. Husbands and wives should be friends to build a lasting marriage. But what does that mean exactly? Does it mean that you both should like the same things or enjoy the same activities? I don't believe it does. But I do think that you need to follow biblical teachings about friendship. God designed marriage to be the most dynamic and intense human relationship of all. He planned image-bearing marriages to be spiritual, physical, romantic, and loving. But he also intended it to grow through friendship.

King Solomon described his spouse as, "… my lover, my friend."[69] The book of Song of Solomon is divinely inspired scripture that serves as a guidebook for romance, love, and biblical marriage. It can also show the relationship between Christ and his bride, the Church. The Bible is extremely practical in nature and never covers up the faults and shortcomings of the men who wrote it. Solomon, while wise and guided by God to write this for us, certainly was not perfect in his marriage. Or maybe I should say in his marriages because he took 700 wives and 300 concubines. That is hard to fathom, but I believe it demonstrates God's grace to us. Even spiritual leaders in the Bible were human, and their lives are on display for us, warts and all.

The Bible teaches that one of the purposes of marriage is a strong bond of friendship. I love the word "companion,"

69 Song of Solomon 5:16, NLT.

which is used to describe a husband or wife in several places throughout the Bible. It means "special confidant" or "best friend." In Genesis 2 God calls Eve a "helper suitable for Adam." It is quite clear that, in addition to being united spiritually and physically, God intends for husbands and wives to connect as companions and friends. What can we learn about befriending each other?

Friends Commit

Throughout this book, I have referred to the Genesis story of the first marriage between Adam and Eve. From it, we get valuable principles for friendship. We see the most compelling, intense sort of human connection. God designed marriage to be a spiritual, physical, romantic, and loving relationship that is held together by a strong friendship. God said that the two were to be united and they were to become one flesh. This union is no fair-weather friendship that leaves whenever things get tough. A bond of this nature demands loyalty, forgiveness, love, and commitment. When I see marriage through the lens of the gospel, I remember that Jesus never gave up on me so I must never give up on my spouse!

Friends are Honest

Before they sinned, Adam and Eve remained open and honest with each other. They had no hidden secrets. They talked openly and shared deeply. That is what friends do. They are honest and transparent with each other. The

New Testament speaks of confessing our faults to each other, supporting each other, encouraging each other, and, when necessary, confronting each other in love. Married people must commit to honesty and openness. Only marriages that rest on this principle have the foundation to last.

Friends Share a Common Vision

Friends share at least one similar taste, which causes them to like each other. You can find a common passion with another person over football. That mutual interest can even develop into a friendship. It may or may not go any deeper than that, but you have a shared enthusiasm, therefore, a reason to become acquainted. The Apostle Peter wrote, "Finally, all of you should be of one mind. Sympathize with each other. Love each other… "[70] The word "sympathize" means "to have a common passion." Being of one mind means that we should have the same vision for our lives. We must head toward the same target. The best way to become friends with your spouse is to share a common passion for loving Jesus and serving Him. You must also share similar goals for training your children. Your approach may be different, but you must agree on the desired outcome. Share a collective vision for your marriage, children, future, and retirement, so you arrive at the same destination.

70 1 Peter 3:8.

Friends Help Each Other

God called Eve a suitable helper for Adam. They helped each other in many ways, but perhaps the most important way was spiritual in nature. If God had the gospel in mind when He fashioned marriage, then we must strive to help our spouse spiritually. How do you do that? You must commit to helping each other grow in Christ. The only way to accomplish this is to keep Jesus at the center of your marriage.

Marriage mirrors our relationship with Christ. We can't understand it's purpose without looking at the gospel. In the biblical narrative, Jesus did not die to make bad people good, but to make dead people live. If the metaphor holds, then having a Jesus-centered marriage means that He did not come to make your bad marriage better, but to make your dead marriage live! Christ died and rose again to change you and make you alive in Him. He brings dead things back to life! Only when you begin to understand the gospel can you begin to know how to be a genuine friend to your spouse. The secret to befriending your spouse is to be committed to assisting with his or her next step with Jesus. Friendship is ultimately about helping others grow in their relationship with Christ.

Talk with Your Wife

1. *Describe to your spouse what you think about your friendship with each other.*
2. *Talk about your vision or goals for your marriage.*
3. *Talk about your vision or goals for your children.*
4. *Ask how you can help your spouse grow closer to Jesus.*
5. *Pray and ask God to bless your friendship with your spouse.*

DAY TWENTY-EIGHT

Overcoming the Consumer Mentality

When Kim and I were first married, we slept like a pretzel. I thought that was a requirement. We did not know that much about each other, especially when it came to sleeping habits. I soon discovered that she is a cold sleeper. She likes lots of covers and loves to sleep burrowed under blankets to keep her warm. I, on the other hand, am a hot sleeper. I sweat and toss and turn and dream violent dreams. It makes it nearly impossible for anyone to sleep while touching me. After a few months of not sleeping well, Kim blurted out one night, "Stop touching me! I can't sleep!" I was relieved, and so was she. We have slept just fine ever since.

Change is inevitable in you. I am different than I was when I was twenty-one years old. So are you. Because we always change throughout our lives, we must learn how to stay in love with our spouse over time. To survive the inevitable differences, you must make a commitment to love each other no matter what changes in your lives. You must learn to stop consuming and start committing.

We live in a consumer culture. If something displeases us, then we move on to another product, another store, another restaurant, or even another marriage. Unfortunately, many Christians treat their relationship with the church as a consumer. Rather than being deeply committed and serving sacrificially, they sink shallow roots and are on the lookout for the next new thing.

The Consumer Model

When you are a consumer, you are open to other options. If something newer, more exciting, or more pleasing comes along, then you will leave your old model and get a new one. If your old model displeases you, then you will get rid of it and get a new one. We do this with phones, restaurants, and, unfortunately, spouses. A consumer mentality means that we prioritize what we get from something, not what we bring to something. Let me illustrate.

My wife and I took a trip to Florida several years ago. We stopped for gas at a cool-looking store that offered all kinds of specialty foods from the local area. Many of their products came from Georgia pecans. I love pecan pie, so it made sense to stop there. I filled our car with gas and went inside the store to browse. After selecting several high-calorie food options, I went to the cashier to pay for my gas and the delectable delights that I could not wait to devour. We were the only people in the store except for the cashier. When I tried to pay, the cashier told me that I could not purchase my gas and food at the same cash register. She informed me that I must pay for my gas at one register, and then pay for my snacks at another. Then she stared at me like I was trying to steal a candy bar. I realize that I am a Christian. I am also a pastor. Most people do not let such silly things upset them. But I never claimed to be normal. It frustrated me so much that I paid for my gas and left my tasty delights on the counter. I went on to inform the lady that I would never visit her establishment again. I told her if I were to run out of gas next to her store, then I would walk ten miles rather than to buy gas or anything else from her store. I have never stopped at her store again. I realize how silly that is, but I just can't bring myself to buy anything from her because of the way she made me feel. That is what I mean by having a consumer mentality.

The consumer model demands options. It responds based on feelings rather than principles. The priority becomes what the other person can do for you. It sees love only as an emotion from which our actions flow. It rejects the biblical definition of love as a deed first, followed by a feeling later. Godly love is active through service and self-sacrifice. The worldly definition of love slowly ruins a marriage. Consumer-based love depends on circumstances. If your feelings change, then you feel free to abandon the marriage. Many Christians build their marriage on the consumer model. As a result, they never discover the bond of true love that God wants for them. They never feel the joy of commitment. They never experience sustained marital happiness.

The Commitment Model

Marital love is only able to grow stronger over time when it is rooted in the commitment model. I do not mean to suggest that emotions and attraction are unimportant. The Bible teaches that passion and desire are only able to flourish when coupled with commitment. God tells us that we are to "cleave" to one another.[71] It means we are to stick together, like glue. The Bible uses the word "cleave" to describe an oath, a covenant, a binding promise, or a vow.

God does not say that desire, romance, and emotions are unimportant. God created these desires. Read the book of Song of Solomon, and you will discover that God wants your marriage to be romantic and erotic. In that short book, the husband talks about his wife's beauty, her eyes, her hair, her breasts, her lips, her breath, how her lips taste, how her tongue tastes, her thighs, her belly, and her "garden." If you wonder what he means when he describes her garden, then let me tell you that he is not talking about a bean patch! Some people think the Bible is boring! Stop reading romance novels and start reading the Bible if you want to learn about love.

Jesus commanded us to love our spouse, our neighbor, and our enemies. You cannot command an emotion. I once saw a mom demand that her kids be happy because she "paid a lot of money for this stinking amusement park." Nice try. Evidently, Jesus charged us to have loving actions rather than loving feelings. In the Bible, emotions follow actions. Commitment creates fertile soil for love. Love consists of self-sacrificing actions; therefore, it is not dependent on circumstances. Biblical love is not about self-fulfillment but self-sacrifice. Loving with your actions enables your feelings to follow. A commitment to loving action overcomes the inevitable emotional swings in a marriage and

71 Genesis 2:24-25.

keeps us committed to each other. If you stay committed, your marriage will grow, and your emotions will deepen and mature over time. When we love our spouse as Jesus loves us, we find acceptance, security, and lasting love.

My hope for you is that you find the courage and faith to commit to the biblical model of love. God's love will empower you to stop being a consumer and to start following the example that Jesus gave us.

Talk with Your Wife

1. *Talk about the consumer mentality that permeates our culture. How can you avoid that mentality in your marriage?*
2. *What are some ways that a strong commitment to each other helps your love to grow?*
3. *Tell your wife some positive changes that have happened in your life since you married her.*
4. *Think of two things you can do for your spouse that are loving actions and do them. How does this make you feel?*
5. *Pray that God will deepen your commitment to Jesus and each other.*

DAY TWENTY-NINE

Capturing and Keeping Your Wife's Heart

Drink water from your own cistern,
flowing water from your own well.
Should your springs be scattered abroad,
streams of water in the streets?

Let them be for yourself alone,

and not for strangers with you.

Let your fountain be blessed,

and rejoice in the wife of your youth,

a lovely deer, a graceful doe.

Let her breasts fill you at
all times with delight;

be intoxicated always in her love.[72]
King Solomon of Israel

Solomon said some amazing things about marriage. I don't suggest having 700 wives and 300 concubines, but there is no record that shows he got divorced. One thing that caught my eye in that passage was the word "intoxicated." He was not suggesting that you may need alcohol to survive your marriage. Think of these synonyms for intoxicated or intoxicating; merry, happy, mind-altering,

72 Proverbs 5:15-19, ESV.

exciting, invigorating, and strong. Are those words that you would like associated with your relationship?

Intoxicated people are emotionally available, generous, and uninhibited by fear. Feeling inebriated is an experience that once you have had it, you want to have it again. There are several principles in these verses that will help you capture and keep the heart of your spouse.

Spend Time Together

Nobody ever gets married thinking that they will not spend much time together. But life has a funny way of getting in the way. The point is that if you don't pay attention to each other and spend time together, then you may come home one day only to find your barrel empty.

You must be intentional about spending time together. It will not happen by accident. Couples who thrive and stay in love make spending quality time together a priority. Have a regular date each week. Get someone to watch your kids and spend time together so that you can grow closer.

Learn to Enjoy Each Other

There is something magical about taking delight in each other's body, as Solomon so aptly wrote. God created marriage to bring us much joy and pleasure. Find joy in the Lord and each other. God suggests a "hands-on" experience. When you strive to find happiness and satisfaction in your spouse, then you naturally tend to enjoy his or her company, personality, eccentricities, and physical presence. Find ways to serve each other and make each other feel wanted. Spend lots of time "delighting" in each other.

Don't Take Your Marriage for Granted

One of the most difficult things to do in a relationship is to keep apathy from creeping in. You must be intentional about *not taking each other for granted.* Have a conversation tonight and search out the ways you have taken each other for granted and vow to work on doing better.

Build a Wall of Protection

Don't stumble into an affair or a divorce. Most people never cheat on purpose. No one ever enters marriage thinking that they will get divorced. But if you do not pay attention to detail, then slowly but surely apathy will creep into your relationship. Set up boundaries and guard your thoughts and marriage. Filter your relationships at work. Guard the media you consume. Protect your mind by filling it with the Bible. By taking delight in each other and rejoicing in each other, you are building a wall of protection around your marriage.

Make sure that you maintain the discipline required to guard your heart. Although we do not usually associate discipline with romance, we should. According to what Solomon wrote, marriage takes work and discipline. You can build a powerfully intoxicating marriage if you will just work at it!

Live for a Greater Purpose

Many families attend church together, but families that serve together are the strongest. The truest delight comes from serving God as a family. When you have the same goal of serving God and living for His purpose, then you find joy. You can have different career goals, financial goals, and educational goals, but you must share the common purpose of living for God and pleasing Him to intoxicate the heart of your spouse.

Express Yourself

Solomon declared his love freely. You must not be afraid to communicate your love to your wife. Not to do so violates the way God created you. When Adam saw Eve for the first time he openly expressed his awe. He unabashedly shouted his emotions. God had just created Eve and brought her to Adam. She was beautiful, vulnerable, and they were both naked. You can imagine that he was excited to see a woman after having looked at the animals for so long. I believe his reaction was much deeper than the primal urges a man feels when he sees a beautiful, naked woman. It is a reaction that shows great vulnerability, great openness, and great oneness. He knew that God created them to be together, and he was going to love this woman deeply. So, he exuberantly told her. Adam waxed poetic and quoted the first romance line in the history of the world. He expressed himself and did not care what anyone else thought. Every woman since loves to hear a man express himself to the point of embarrassment.

Be bold in expressing your love to your wife. Adam was. So was Solomon. Their example gives us a way to capture and keep the heart of the women we love.

Talk with Your Wife

1. *How is your date night? Do you spend time each week with each other away from the kids?*
2. *What are some ways that you can enjoy each other and delight in each other?*
3. *How are your barriers? Have you set up boundaries at work and on social media?*
4. *Express yourself. Tell your wife at least three ways she brings you joy.*
5. *Pray that God will put a barrier around your marriage and that you will find intoxication in each other.*

DAY THIRTY

Advice for Developing a Love That Lasts

Congratulations on making it to the last day of your thirty-day journey to a better marriage. I hope you have learned to love each other more. Here are a few final thoughts and principles that will help you have a stronger marriage.

Be Yourself

I once asked a man who had been married for over 50 years what was his secret to a long and happy marriage. With a twinkle in his eye, he looked at me for a long, uncomfortable moment. I could not tell if he was thinking back on his early romantic escapades with his young bride or if he was having a senior moment, and was trying to recall who I was. Finally, he said, "The secret, son, is this. For many years, my wife and I faithfully lived by this one principle. We did not let anything get in the way of fulfilling it every week. We went out twice a week without fail. I went out on Fridays, and she went out on Saturdays."

I am not sure if that is the best advice I have ever heard or not, but it worked for them. One of the temptations we face in our culture is the temptation to compare. If we compare ourselves to others, then we lose. It is tempting to read about people on social media or to watch people's lives on TV and think that our life is somehow lacking. Don't fall into that trap. Learn to accept your life as a gift from God. He made you with the ability and personality that brings glory to Him. Be okay with being you. And stop comparing your life to what you see on social media. What you see is heavily edited and never tells the whole story.

Learn Your Communication Rhythms

Sometimes the reason communication breaks down is that we do not choose the right time or environment. Find out if your spouse is ready or not to talk immediately when he or she gets home. Some people need to unwind first before they talk. Couples who do not learn how to communicate with each other at the right time and in the right way will end up frustrated. Solomon gave wonderful advice on how to find your rhythm in three helpful verses:

> "Intelligent people think before they speak; what they say then is more persuasive."[73]
>
> "The right word at the right time is like precious gold set in silver."[74]
>
> "A wise mature person is known for his understanding. The more pleasant his words the more persuasive he is."[75]

Avoid sarcasm, belittling, and abrasive talk at all costs because they are conversation killers. Don't force conversation or use negative language, negative body language, or

73 Proverbs 16:23, GNB.

74 Proverbs 25:11, CEV.

75 Proverbs 16:21, GNB.

unfair generalizations. "You always" or "You never" probably should be eliminated from your vocabulary. Learn how your spouse receives communication. Sometimes it is not what we say but how we say it that matters. You must always be willing to forgive to keep open the lines of communication.

Remember that time together is necessary for good communication. A good conversation happens best in the natural flow of relaxed time together. Be generous with eye contact, focused attention, and personal touch. Sometimes just a hug, a touch on the arm, an arm around the shoulder, or holding hands can do wonders for your communication. Be generous with the praise as well. It will do wonders for your marriage.

Get Help

Don't be afraid to get help. Talk to someone. After years of marriage and ministry, I have concluded that every couple needs to get counseling. Kim and I have received help from friends, mentors, therapists, psychologists, and psychiatrists, and we are proud of it! I used to think that counseling was only for weak people. I could not have been more wrong. At some point, you will need help. Talk to a counselor. Counsel with a pastor. Speak to someone in your small group or an older couple at church. You get coaching and training for your job, a hobby, a sport, for driving an automobile, and many other things. Don't hesitate to get training for your marriage. It will make your marriage stronger and your life better.

Men, there it is – marriage in the nude. I hope you grow in love and grace. I hope that you begin taking steps toward the kind of marriage God intended for you. I hope you find love for a lifetime. I hope you will get naked and stay naked with your wife.

Talk with Your Wife

1. *Talk about your communication rhythms.*
2. *How can you both get better at communicating with each other?*
3. *Do you think you need coaching for your marriage? Who can you talk to about it?*
4. *How has this book helped you?*
5. *Pray for God to give you a stronger marriage.*

Ritchie Miller is a pastor, teacher, and author with a passion for reaching this generation for Christ. He is the founding and Senior Pastor of Avalon Church and travels throughout the world teaching, training pastors, supporting missionary and educational endeavors, and planting churches. Ritchie and his wife, Kim, live in Georgia and have three adult children, Brittney, Brandon, and Brooke.

For more information about Ritchie, to read his blog, to listen to his sermons, or to connect with him, go to www.ritchiemiller.org or to www.avalonchurch.net. You can follow him on Twitter @ritchiemillerGA or on Facebook.

Made in the USA
Columbia, SC
16 July 2017